Reforming Land-Use Planning: Property Rights Approaches

John Corkindale

Published by the IEA Environment Unit, 1998

First published in July 1998 by
The Environment Unit
The Institute of Economic Affairs
2 Lord North Street
Westminster
London SW1P 3LB

IEA Studies on the Environment No. 12
All rights reserved
ISBN 0-255 36446-6

Many IEA publications are translated into languages other than English or are reprinted. Permission to translate or to reprint should be sought from the General Director at the address above.

Printed in Great Britain by
Hartington Fine Arts Limited, Lancing, West Sussex
Set in Times New Roman and Univers

Contents

	Foreword *Julian Morris*	7
	The Authors	11
	Acknowledgements	12
1.	**Introduction**	**13**
	Economic Evaluation of the Planning System	14
	The Nationalisation of Land Development Rights	17
	The Rôle of the Courts	18
2.	**The Objectives of Land-Use Planning**	**20**
	Urban Containment	21
	Optimal City Size	23
	Urban Sprawl	24
	Coping with Projected Growth in Household Formation	25
	Technological and Pecuniary Externalities	26
	Public Goods	27
	Sustainable Development	28
3.	**Property Rights, Economics and Planning**	**32**
	The Evolution of Property Rights and the Rôle of the Common Law	32
	The Normative Economic Theory of Property	33
	Liability Rules and Property Rules	36
	Easements and Covenants	36
	The Polluter Pays Principle	37

4.	The Privatisation of Land Development Rights	40
	The Economics of Privatisation	40
	Land-Use Planning in Ontario	43
	The User Pays Principle in Land-Use Planning	45

5.	Zoning and Tradable Development Rights	48
	Economic Evaluation of Zoning	49
	Market-Based Instruments	51
	Tradable Permits v. Emission Charges	52
	Tradable Development Rights	53
	The Habitat Transaction Method	54
	Tradable Development Rights in the United Kingdom?	55

6.	Conclusion: Time to Privatise Land-Development Rights	56
	References	58
	Glossary	65

Commentary by Malcolm Grant	69
Introduction	69
The Overall Approach	70
The Objectives of the Planning System	70
The Internalisation of Technological Externalities	71
The Articulation of Objectives	73
The Provision of Public Goods	75
Models of Privatisation of Development Rights	76

Conclusions	82
Commentary by Mark Pennington	84
Summary	*Back Cover*

Foreword

A few years ago I had dinner with a foreign expert in land-use planning who was at that time carrying out research at Aberdeen University. After a while the discussion turned to his academic interest and I inquired as to his opinion of the British planning system. He said he found it interesting but rather complicated. Intrigued, I asked how he thought it compared to the system in his country. He replied that the land-use planning system in his country was certainly not great but it was better than the one here because it was more flexible – it was better able to deal with the changing desires of the population. He came from China.

The problems associated with obtaining planning permission will be well known to anyone who has ever tried to make any substantial changes to their home or, perish the thought, tried to build on undeveloped land. For those who are not so familiar, the following case will perhaps serve to illustrate the point.

On 20 July 1988 the South Lakeland District Council received an application from the Carlisle diocesan parsonages board for permission to erect a new vicarage on a site within the Cartmel Conservation Area. On 12 September 1988 the council rejected the application on the grounds that:

> 'The proposal would be seriously detrimental to the history, architecture and visual character of this part of the Cartmel Conservation Area and would be contrary to policies C5 and C23 of the Cartmel and Furness Local Plan and C14/C15 of the Cumbria and Lake District Joint Structure Plan, First Alteration.'

On 9 March 1989 the parsonages board appealed to the Secretary of State for the Environment against the refusal of permission. The Secretary of State appointed an inspector to determine the appeal. On 13 July 1989 the appeal was allowed but six weeks later the district council applied for the decision to be quashed. The application was successful and the Secretary of State appealed.

Finally, on 12 March 1991, more than two and a half years after the initial application was made, the Court of Appeal allowed the appeal and the development was thereby permitted.[1]

This case highlights one of the substantial unseen costs of the planning system, namely the very great delay that can occur between deciding to make some alteration to one's property and the eventual granting of permission. The situation for the person whose application for planning permission is eventually refused is obviously worse, although the great costs of taking legal action mean that many people will simply not bother to appeal against a planning decision that goes against them.

The case also highlights the problems of attempting to develop objective criteria for resolving aesthetic conflicts. Each of us views the world with different eyes. Where one person sees a beautiful modernist building another sees a brutalist monstrosity; where one sees a fine example of neo-classical architecture another sees a kitsch pastiche; where one sees a patchwork of fields another sees cereal crops interspersed with hedges. How then can we all live at peace? Should certain aesthetic decisions be elevated to a higher authority? Which decisions should be considered so important that they should be so elevated? What criteria should that authority employ to make those aesthetic decisions? In the context of land-use planning: what criteria should the higher authority use to decide what may be built and what may be demolished?

In this regard, it is perhaps instructive to consider the response of the inspector appointed to evaluate the plans for another proposed development in a Conservation Area:[2]

> 'The design of the proposed building has been criticised for being incorrect within the grammar of classical design or, at least, idiosyncratic in its use of Classical elements. The architect has certainly used the elements of the Classical vocabulary in a free, and in some respects, non-traditional way, but the resulting building is not unpleasing nor out of character with its setting ... the proposed building would be appropriate to its site and setting. It represents a

---

[1] *South Lakeland DC v Secretary of State for the Environment* [1992] 1 All ER 573, per Mann LJ.

[2] *Bath Society v Secretary of State for the Environment* [1992] 1 All ER 28.

successful attempt to design in harmony with classical principles, but without slavish adherence to precedent.'[3]

This book is intended to set the ball rolling in a debate over reform of planning law. Questions to be answered include the following. What rights should individuals have in respect of land-use development? If individuals' rights are to be limited, at what level of aggregation should decisions about permissible development take place? Are the current objectives of land-use planning reasonable? Are the costs associated with the planning system worthwhile in terms of the benefits that accrue? What other objectives might land-use planners apply in addition to or instead of the current objectives? What is the appropriate relation between land-use planning and provision of environmental amenities?

John Corkindale's analysis focuses on three main issues. *First*, he assesses the current system and notes that the primary rôle of land-use planning since the war has been to constrain urban development. Using economic analysis, he argues that such an objective has little merit. *Second*, he suggests alternative objectives for a system of land-use planning which would focus on the 'technological externalities' created by development. *Third*, he proposes alternatives that might be used in place of the current system of development controls, including the introduction of systems of tradable development rights and more democratically accountable mechanisms for setting planning rules.

In their commentaries, both Malcolm Grant and Mark Pennington praise Mr Corkindale for providing fresh impetus to the planning debate. However, Professor Grant is 'unconvinced both by the diagnosis and the prescription' offered by Mr Corkindale. In part, he explains, this is because of a lack of thorough development of the policy prescriptions that are discussed, and he offers several suggestions as to how such

---

[3] *Ibid.* In that case (heard only a month before *South Lakeland*), the decision to grant permission was quashed by the Court of Appeal on the grounds that (1) insufficient consideration had been given to the local plan inspector's recommendation that part of the site to be developed should remain open space – which was a 'material consideration', and (2) although the planning inspector had concluded that the impact of the development 'would not be unacceptably great', the Court found that it would nevertheless not preserve the appearance of the conservation area.

development might progress. However, Professor Grant is in agreement with Mr Corkindale about some aspects of the current system: 'There is indeed a good case for improving the mechanisms for private law to enable private agreements to resolve land-use disputes at neighbour nuisance level, and to allow the state to withdraw from its current local land-use mediation rôle and obsession with loft extensions, granny annexes and running businesses from home' (p. 73).

Mark Pennington seems more convinced by the general thrust of Mr Corkindale's analysis, but is similarly critical of the policy prescriptions − arguing that whilst the introduction of tradable development rights would be an improvement over the current situation, it is not a true market solution. Dr Pennington briefly adumbrates such a solution, emphasising the rôle of private restrictive covenants as a means of ensuring protection of particular aesthetic values.

As with all Institute publications, the views expressed in this monograph are those of the authors, not of the Institute (which has no corporate view), its Trustees, Advisors, or Directors. It is published as an important contribution to the debate on land-use policy.

June 1998   *JULIAN MORRIS*
Assistant Director, Environment Unit

The Authors

John Corkindale graduated from University College, Durham, in economics and economic history and subsequently took a post-graduate diploma in agricultural economics at Cambridge University. On completion of his studies, he was appointed an Overseas Development Institute/Nuffield Fellow and worked at the Ministry of Agriculture, Nairobi, Kenya. On returning to the UK, he held economic advisory posts in the Department of Employment, HM Treasury, and the Northern Ireland Department of Finance and Personnel, Belfast.

Following a brief period of conservation planning for the Royal Society for the Protection of Birds, Mr Corkindale returned to London from Northern Ireland at the end of 1987. He was subsequently employed as economic advisor by the Department of the Environment with responsibilities for the economics of biodiversity conservation and land-use planning. In 1995, he was awarded a government research fellowship which he took up at the Department of Land Economy, Cambridge University. He now operates on a freelance basis.

Malcolm Grant is Professor of Land Economy at Cambridge, and a Professorial Fellow of Clare College. He has been for many years the Editor of the *Encyclopedia of Planning Law and Practice*, and has written and advised extensively in planning and environmental law. He is Chairman of the Local Government Commission for England and a consultant to Eversheds, solicitors.

Mark Pennington was awarded his PhD in September 1997. His research interests are focused on property rights solutions to environmental problems and public choice theory, both of which are exemplified in his thesis 'Property Rights, Public Choice & the Containment of Urban England'. Dr Pennington is currently employed as a research fellow in the Department of Geography

& Environment at the London School of Economics and has been a research fellow at the IEA Environment Unit since March 1995. He is the author of *Conservation and the Countryside: By Quango or Market?* (IEA Studies on the Environment, No. 6, 1996).

Acknowledgements

The background research for this paper was carried out whilst I was a visiting government research fellow at the Department of Land Economy, Cambridge University. I should like to acknowledge the financial support I received during this time from the Cabinet Office and the (then) Department of the Environment. I should also like to thank Malcolm Grant and Peter Tyler of the Department of Land Economy for enabling me to make use of the University's facilities, and the other staff of the Department for providing practical help and intellectual stimulus.

A number of people has been most helpful in the preparation of this paper, but it is right that I should single out, in particular, Malcolm Grant and Mark Pennington, who as well as providing published comments below, commented in some detail on an earlier draft. Also, Julian Morris acted as editor and made innumerable helpful suggestions to improve the presentation of the argument; his input has been absolutely invaluable.

The responsibility for any errors in the text is, of course, mine.

J.C.
May 1998

1. Introduction

The British land-use planning system has now been in place for fifty years and the conventional wisdom is that it is here to stay.[1] The UK Department of the Environment has claimed that the town and country planning system has served the country well and that it is an important instrument for protecting and enhancing the environment in town and country, preserving both built and natural heritage (PPG1, 1992, paragraph 2).[2] This claim invites a number of important questions: Just how well has the planning system served the country? What are the criteria against which success and failure can be assessed? What scope is there for improvements to the system? What alternative options for improvement can be identified? What are the advantages and disadvantages, costs and benefits of these various options? Who gains and who loses from them? More fundamentally, what does it mean to say that the town and country system has served the country well? Does it mean that those people who operate the system work hard and conscientiously? Does it mean that they are successful in dealing quickly and efficiently with their work? Does it mean that the planning system successfully delivers planning objectives as specified in the Planning Policy Guidance Notes? Does it mean that these objectives are being delivered in a cost-effective manner? Are the objectives themselves sensible? Are they consistent or mutually contradictory? Is it possible to measure progress towards them?

---

[1] The current system derives from the 1947 Town and Country Planning Acts and subsequent legislation. The system is governed by different legislation in Scotland, but operates in an essentially similar manner throughout Great Britain. The legislation has been amended on a number of occasions, most notably by the 1991 Planning and Compensation Act, which introduced the concept of 'plan-led development'.

[2] The general principles under which the planning system operates in England and Wales are set out in Planning Policy Guidance Note 1 (PPG1), first published in January 1988 and subsequently revised and amended to reflect legislative changes and developments in policy stemming, in particular, from the Environment White Paper, 'This Common Inheritance' (Cmnd. 1200) published in September 1990. The most recent version of PPG1 was published in February 1997. More detailed policy guidance is to be found principally in other Planning Policy Guidance Notes (PPGs), Minerals Planning Guidance Notes (MPGs), and Regional Planning Guidance Notes (RPGs).

It hardly needs to be said that there are many circumstances under which the town and country planning system might not serve the country well. It might not do so if the people who operate the system work hard and conscientiously but nevertheless fail to deal effectively with their work. It might not do so if the satisfactory completion of this work does not result in progress towards the achievement of the planning system's objectives. It certainly will not do so if the objectives themselves are not sensible ones. And so on. The point is that the claim that the town and country planning system has served the country well is a judgement that can only be made with conviction if it is based on a systematic analysis of the relevant facts, including, in particular, a proper assessment of whose interests are advanced and whose suppressed by the operation of the planning system. In the absence of such an analysis such a claim can all too easily seem, at best, complacent and, at worst, simply wrong.

Economic Evaluation of the Planning System

Several attempts have been made to evaluate the British land-use planning system using economic analysis (Harrison, 1977; Willis, 1980; PIEDA, 1992). Yet for various reasons the impact of these efforts on planning policy has been limited. One important factor has been the failure of land-use planners and economists to speak the same language, each using different criteria to judge particular outcomes. Alan Evans (1985) suggests that two very different criteria are being applied. The first is the sense in which the Apollo programme to land a man on the moon was a success: the cost is largely irrelevant, and success is equated with the achievement of the objective. The second is the sense in which a business is successful: its product is in demand at a price that allows the business to continue to be profitable. It is the second criterion with which the economic analyst is concerned.[3]

---

[3] Of course, the economist engaged in the evaluation of land-use planning policy is not seeking to answer questions about the profitability of land use as such, but, in essence, he is not asking a different sort of question from that being asked by the accountant of a private firm. Rather, he is asking the same sort of question about a wider group of people - who comprise society as a whole (Mishan, 1971). Instead of asking whether the owners of the enterprise will become better off by the firm engaging in one activity rather than another, the economist asks whether society as a whole will

The principal justification for bringing economic analysis to bear on the problem of land use is that land is a scarce resource and that economics is the study of the allocation of scarce resources between competing human wants (Robbins, 1932). The importance of making progress in the economic evaluation of the land-use planning system derives partly from the costs involved – both direct and indirect. The direct costs of running the system are real enough; for the United Kingdom as a whole these are currently of the order of £1 billion per annum.[4] As regards the indirect costs, economists have analysed the implications of the planning system on land and house prices (Eve, 1992; Cheshire and Sheppard, 1989, 1996; Bramley and Watkins, 1996). Cheshire and Sheppard made use of comparative data from Reading and Darlington to examine what the impact on housing development and house prices in Reading might have been had the local planning authority adopted the more relaxed planning régime found in Darlington.[5] The results suggested that plot sizes would have been 65 per cent bigger and the area of the town 50 per cent bigger, because people living in the area would have been able to afford larger housing with bigger gardens. Land prices in Reading would have fallen considerably and real incomes risen commensurately.[6]

There is also concern – but little research – that the planning system is imposing a burden on business. Controls on the development of green field sites, particularly in Green Belts, lead to high land prices in those areas and may result in the diversion of investment to locations less favoured by business or even the loss of prospective investment altogether. In addition, the excessive

---

become better off by taking a particular land-use planning decision rather than by not taking it, or by taking instead any of a number of alternative decisions. Whatever the reason, it remains the case that, despite the fact that it is now half a century since the 1947 Town and Country Planning Acts became law, the British land-use planning system has not been the subject of sustained economic evaluation (B. J. Pearce, 1992).

[4] It is now routine to charge for planning applications and, consequently, the net public expenditure costs of running the land-use planning system are less than the gross costs.

[5] The two towns were chosen because they differed in the degree of planning restrictiveness but were 'similar' in many other respects.

[6] The impact on household incomes in Reading was estimated to be between £640 per household per annum or 6 per cent of household income at the urban periphery and £775 per household per annum or 8 per cent of household income at the urban core.

bureaucracy associated with the planning system may impose delays, and therefore costs, on business, either directly through the time spent in processing planning applications, or indirectly because of the delays to new public infrastructure investment.

However costly the planning system may or may not be, the important question for planning policy purposes is how these costs compare with the benefits of the system, and it is concern about the benefits of planning that is the other reason for wishing to carry out an economic evaluation. If the costs were clearly shown to be outweighed by the benefits, rather than vice versa, the policy implications would obviously be very different. Unfortunately, estimating the benefits of planning is even more difficult than estimating the costs. The problem is made more severe by the intractable nature of some of the questions, such as the counterfactual 'What would have happened in the absence of the Town and Country Planning Acts?' or 'What would have happened under an entirely different régime?'.

Doubts have been expressed about the extent of the benefits being delivered by the British land-use planning system. For example, Alan Evans (1988) wryly comments on the paradoxical attitude of the British middle classes:

> 'Those who travel outside Britain do not seem to think that the landscapes of Tuscany, Umbria, Brittany or the Loire Valley have been irretrievably ruined by piecemeal development. On the contrary, they seem to be pleased that villas and gites exist which are relatively cheap and which allow them to live in rural surroundings.'

Compare this with the advice contained in the Department of the Environment's planning guidance on the countryside and the rural economy (PPG7), which requires that 'the expansion of villages and towns must avoid creating ribbon development or a fragmented pattern of development' and that 'new housebuilding and other new development in the open countryside, away from established settlements, should be strictly controlled'. Evidently, 'the fact that a single house on a particular site would be unobtrusive' is not by itself a good argument; it could be 'repeated too often', although precisely what constitutes 'too often' and against what criteria are not spelled out.

Given the practical difficulties associated with measuring the costs and benefits of the British system of land-use planning, we shall not dwell on these issues here. Our purpose is, rather, to discuss how efficiency improvements might be achieved, thereby increasing the net benefits from land use. In order to do this, a first step is to inquire a little more closely into the way in which the British land-use planning system currently operates.

The Nationalisation of Land Development Rights

Under the terms of the Town and Country Planning Acts, the general position is that anyone who wishes to develop land by carrying out a substantial physical operation or by making any significant change to the use of land or buildings must first obtain planning permission from the local planning authority (LPA). If that authority refuses planning permission or imposes conditions which are unacceptable to the prospective developer, the latter may appeal to the appropriate government minister: in England this is now the Secretary of State for the Environment, Transport and the Regions.

The owner of the value added by planning permission is, of course, a crucial issue and, in Britain, this has largely been at the whim of the political administration of the day. The 1947 Acts introduced a 100 per cent development charge or 'tax on betterment'. The Acts made a sharp distinction between the profits to be made out of rising land values and the profits to be made out of organising the construction process. They assumed the former to be 'unethical', but the latter they saw as perfectly legitimate (Reade, 1987). The development charge was abolished by the Conservative administration in 1953. In 1967, the Labour administration introduced a 40 per cent tax on betterment, but this was again repealed by the incoming Conservative administration in 1971. In 1976, the Labour administration introduced betterment taxation at rates varying from 66.6 per cent to 80 per cent on betterment in excess of £10,000. In 1980, the Conservative administration raised this threshold to £50,000 and introduced a single top rate of 60 per cent. In 1985, it abolished the tax altogether.

The identity of the owner of the development value affects our view of the impact of land-use planning on those who are refused the right to develop their land. If development value belongs to the state, then it follows that those who are prevented from developing their land should not be compensated. If, on the other hand, development value is the property of owners or developers, then those who are not permitted to realise it should be compensated, and there can be no 'tax' or recoupment of this development value by the state (Reade, 1987). Under the current system, the land owner has no automatic right to develop his land or even change its use – to do so he must obtain permission from the appropriate authorities. Thus, when planning permission is refused, or granted subject to conditions, it is only rarely that the applicant will be entitled to compensation of any kind (Stephen, 1988).[7] The current situation therefore presents something of an ethical contradiction, since development value accrues to the landowner, but those adversely affected by the planning system are rarely compensated. In effect, the Town and Country Planning Acts nationalised land development rights and allowed planning authorities to re-privatise those rights on a partial and discretionary basis.

The Rôle of the Courts

The local planning authority and the Minister have a wide measure of discretion as to whether to grant planning permission and as to the conditions under which that planning permission will be granted. These discretionary powers have, however, been limited by the courts by application of the *ultra vires* doctrine. The courts thus declare unlawful planning decisions which are not authorised by statute or which involve an abuse of a statutory power in the sense that the power has been employed in a manner which, in the court's view, was not intended by Parliament. The courts may quash a planning decision if there has been a failure to consider a material consideration or if some irrelevant factor has been taken into account. There is, however, little statutory guidance as to what are, or are not, 'material considerations'.[8]

---

[7] Under the terms of the 1947 Town and Country Planning Acts, a special compensation fund was set up for the purpose of reimbursing land owners who had lost out as a result of the nationalisation of development rights.

[8] PPG1 specifies that, in principle, any consideration which relates to the use and development of land is capable of a planning consideration. Whether a particular consideration falling within that broad class is 'material' will depend on the

Whilst many planning decisions have been quashed for failure to take account of a material consideration, there have been very few occasions on which the courts have said that a particular consideration is not relevant to planning. Nevertheless, what is a relevant or material consideration is of crucial importance for the system of development control, since it is through this concept that the limits to public intervention in the land-use planning sphere are set (Stephen, 1988).

circumstances. Considerable importance is attached to consistency in determining planning applications. One important material consideration is whether the development plan policies are up-to-date and apply to current circumstances, or whether they have been overtaken by events. For example, policies and proposals in the plan may have been superseded by more recent planning guidance, or developments since the plan became operative may have rendered certain policies or proposals in the plan incapable of implementation or out of date.

The courts are the arbiters of what constitutes a material consideration. All the fundamental factors involved in land-use planning are included, such as the number, size, layout, siting, design and external appearance of buildings and the proposed means of access, together with landscaping, impact on the neighbourhood and the availability of infrastructure.

2. The Objectives of Land-Use Planning

In view of the somewhat draconian powers assumed by government under the provisions of the 1947 Town and Country Planning Acts, it is remarkable how little attempt was made at the time of their passage through Parliament or has been made subsequently to define measurable land-use planning objectives. This was of little surprise to Professor Peter Hall who noted:

'It is small wonder, given the natural tendency to elite government in Britain, that the . . . approach tends to an extremely lofty yet imprecise definition of the public good in terms of ends with infinite values, which are ideologically derived, and are characteristically presented in terms of a concrete set of policy measures . . . There has been little explicit attempt to relate the physically-defined policy objectives – such as urban containment or the protection of rural land – to fundamental objectives related to the value systems of people . . . A very wide variety of public programmes has been allowed to proceed simultaneously, without any systematic attempt to consider whether they were compatible.' (Hall *et al.*, 1973, vol. 2, pp. 69-71).

Hall *et al.* (1973, vol. 2, p. 39) noted that, in practice, the objectives of planning consisted of 'a very short and simple list of criteria', which 'had only the most indirect relevance to any index of welfare' that might be familiar to a social scientist. More recently, a study of the national objectives of the planning system (as specified in the PPGs, etc.) carried out by Cambridge University Department of Land Economy (1995) identified 'a very large array indeed of policy statements which make reference to some desired outcome'.[9] This study found that many of the land-

---

[9] Three levels ('ranks') of objective were categorised:
- broad and general objectives of the 'motherhood and apple pie' variety. These were 'so bland and uncontroversial that it was difficult to see why they had been included . . . how it might be possible to gauge whether or not they had been achieved . . . and sometimes difficult to see what particular rôle the planning system might have had in their achievement';

use planning objectives sought to achieve some standard for the policy object, but that the gap between the present and the desired state of the policy object was rarely made explicit. Neither the extent of the improvement nor the timetable by which it was to be achieved was included. In some cases the objective was couched in terms which sought to move towards some desired standard without a requirement that it actually be achieved. In a few instances the objective simply stated a wish for some improvement on the current position without providing a goal or target to aim at. A particular aspect of this problem concerned the potential conflicts and trade-offs between objectives. A number of policy objectives for the land-use planning system were stated in terms of achieving a balance of objectives, but only rarely were the trade-offs between objectives concerned specified in a way which quantified the 'exchange-rate' between one objective and another.

These deficiencies present particular problems when it comes to evaluating Britain's land-use planning system, since evaluation generally requires precision in the definition of policy objectives. Below, some of the ostensible objectives of planning policy are considered.

Urban Containment

Historically, the principal focus of British planning has been urban containment (Hall *et al.*, 1973), a policy which can be traced back at least to the 1580 proclamation of Queen Elizabeth I that forbade any new building on a site within three miles of the city gates of London (DOE, 1988) and continues today. The 1947 Town and Country Planning Acts were much influenced by discussions of

---

- more specific objectives which clearly lie within the realm of influence of the land-use planning system but which only loosely define the nature of the policy objective. In these cases 'there was some difficulty in being sure of the exact meaning of the policy object';
- policy statements which are 'much more specific and define the nature of the policy objective fairly closely'. There was 'a clear understanding that the desired outcomes were relevant to land-use planning means' and 'the exact nature of the policy object was reasonably clear'. Even at this level, 'very few of the objectives ... were expressed as targets - and where they were, the targets most usually relate[d] to outputs and not outcomes'.

urban containment in a series of official reports produced in the early 1940s. The report of the Royal Commission on the Distribution of Industrial Population (1940), known as the Barlow Report, proposed a strategy for the decentralisation and dispersal of industry and population from the large cities, the redevelopment of the congested centres of these cities, the attainment of balance of industrial development in the regions, and the diversification of industry within each region. The Scott Report on Rural Land Use (1942) favoured the conservation of agricultural land as 'a priceless national asset'. The Abercrombie Greater London Plan (1944) introduced the concept of the development plan. The Reith Report on New Towns (1946) argued that physical planning, as exemplified by new towns, should try to shape the life of the community.[10]

For the most part, the authors of these documents elicited a strong preference for urban containment and a rather rigid distinction between the urban and the rural. The town was seen as artificial, urban; the country, natural, rural (Abercrombie, 1933). Conflict over urban containment is seen most clearly in the Scott Report.[11] In a minority report, Professor Dennison argued that the majority report of the Scott Committee ignored questions of how much was to be paid for preserving rural amenity and who was to pay this price. The objective of the majority of the Scott Committee seems to have been the preservation of a traditional way of life and a traditional economy, whatever the cost (Hall *et al.*, 1973).

Many of the policies designed to 'contain' cities force land into lower-valued uses, leading to higher prices for development land. Yet the policy of preventing development on high-quality agricultural land is simply unnecessary. As in most industrialised

---

[10] The distinction between local development control and the deliberate creation of new and expanded towns also derives from Reith (Hall *et al.*, 1973).

[11] The Scott Committee, in considering the arguments for preserving high and intermediate grade agricultural land, was confronted by a difference of view between the Council for the Protection of Rural England (CPRE) and the Town and Country Planning Association (TCPA). Both organisations were opposed to urban sprawl into the countryside, but, whereas the CPRE emphasised the protection of the countryside for the benefit of the rural population, the TCPA stressed the importance of decentralisation into new towns, the principal beneficiaries of which were likely to be poor people from urban slums.

countries, farmers in the United Kingdom produce huge surpluses because of protectionist agricultural policies. Moreover, in a global economy self-sufficiency in agriculture is neither a necessary nor a desirable goal, since the misallocation of resources that results from attempting to achieve such a goal makes other industries less competitive and reduces overall welfare. Nevertheless, numerous other justifications have been proposed to support urban containment, including the goal of achieving 'Optimal City Size' and constraining 'Urban Sprawl'. These are now considered.

Optimal City Size

At the end of the 19th century, Ebenezer Howard (1898) advocated the concept of the social city that multiplies indefinitely, in a cell-like way, in order to distribute accessibility evenly and so reduce access costs. However, Howard was writing at a time of rapid population growth and he accepted that there would be growth in the extent of urban areas. More recently, demands for reducing access costs have been expressed as the converse of Howard's idea, in the policy of urban containment, which has been advocated on the grounds that it will 'reduce the need to travel'.

It is questionable whether urban containment is worthwhile in transport terms. High-density settlement involves trade-offs between the costs of congestion and the benefits of agglomeration. In most cases, high-rise buildings exist where they do because their developers believed that the returns that would be realised would justify the high costs of erecting and maintaining them. Those high returns are, in turn, generated by the fact that potential occupants are attracted to the superior accessibility, communication, and transactions that their location affords. Over the past century or so, major innovations in transport and communications have changed cities by making the benefits of agglomeration available over increasingly large areas, allowing many of the costs of congestion to be avoided (Gordon and Richardson, 1995).

Some have argued that it is possible, upon weighing the various advantages and disadvantages of large aggregations of population and industry, to define an 'optimal city size' and an optimal number of separate aggregations for the country as a whole. However, it is unlikely that the optimal city size will be the same for cities with different industrial functions; and what is optimal is likely to vary over time with technological change, particularly in transport and communications, with the changing structure of employment and industry, and with rising real incomes and the greater availability of leisure time (Brown, 1972). Structural change of this kind has long been recognised as the embodiment of that economic development upon which we depend for improvements in living standards (Salter, 1963; Wragg and Robertson, 1978).

For most of the 20th century, the development of the road system has been the major force for more low-density settlement and suburbanisation. Factories and offices have been built where employees want to live. Much commuting is suburb to suburb, taking congestion pressures off traditional city centres and allowing many to drive on relatively less congested suburban roads. Rapid advances in telecommunications are contributing to these decentralising trends. The centrifugal trends have accelerated as the range of locational choices open to both households and companies has expanded. In the extreme case, geography might become completely irrelevant; proximity to the work place will become a redundant concept for many as work, particularly office work, will do the travelling rather than the workers (Gordon and Richardson, 1995). In such a dynamic economic and social environment it seems absurd to define and enforce an 'optimal city size'.

Urban Sprawl

Urban containment has also been justified on the grounds that it would prevent 'urban sprawl'. The term urban sprawl is, of course, a pejorative one that has connotations of the general meaning of sprawl as an unaesthetic, lazy, and undisciplined form of body expression. The original application in the planning context was to describe predominantly commercial 'ribbon' development along highways over considerable distances. The term has since been generalised to include almost any kind of low-density suburban and 'leapfrog' development. Whatever the objection to particular kinds of development falling into this general category, it seems inappropriate to extend the argument to suburbanisation *per se*, given the expressed preferences of so many for suburban lifestyles (Gordon and Richardson, 1995).

Coping with Projected Growth in Household Formation

The prospect of growth in numbers of households has clear implications for the viability of a policy of urban containment. It is perhaps unsurprising that the preoccupation with urban containment is central to the 1996 Green Paper 'Household Growth: where shall we live?' (HM Government, 1996), which suggests that there could be up to 4.4 million more households formed in England over the 25-year period 1991 to 2016.[12]

The Green Paper had two purposes. First, it was intended to stimulate debate on whether there is anything that can be done to reduce the rate of household formation, so that it grows more slowly than in recent years. Second, on the assumption that it is necessary to plan for the growth in household numbers more or less in line with the projections, the Green Paper argued that there needs to be a debate on the consequences for the future shape, appearance and operation of the towns and countryside. This debate is to be based on the premise that the growth in households should be used to help regenerate existing towns and cities.

Two basic economic questions arise from the Green Paper. First, Is it necessary to plan for the projected growth in household numbers? Second, If it is necessary to plan for the projected growth, how should this be done? Attempts to provide satisfactory answers to these questions are bedevilled by the policy concern with 'social' or 'affordable' housing. It is not entirely clear how far this has to do with a desire on the part of government to use housing policy as a means of securing a redistribution of income and how far to do with some concept of housing as a 'merit good'. Those questions are beyond the scope of this paper.[13] Suffice it to

---

[12] Part of this growth is accounted for by population growth, but the Green Paper gives three main additional reasons:

1. improved living standards and better health mean people are living longer and often on their own;

2. people are better off and they can afford to set up separate households more easily;

3. changes in social behaviour and attitudes, especially towards marriage and the family, lead to a smaller proportion of households consisting of married couples with children.

[13] The purpose of 'affordable housing' is to substitute for what used to be known as council housing. The idea is that affordable housing is to be provided by developers

say, however, that the availability of subsidised housing will tend to generate more demand for housing and therefore to increase development pressures.

Technological and Pecuniary Externalities

Instead of asking 'How many new houses need to be provided?' or 'Where shall all these new houses be built?' perhaps a more productive question for the Green Paper would have been 'How can the environmental externalities associated with new housing development be most efficiently internalised?' An externality has been defined as a cost or benefit that the voluntary actions of one or more people impose or confer on a third party or parties without their consent (Cooter and Ulen, 1988). It is usual to distinguish between technological and pecuniary externalities (Viner, 1931), especially in the context of land use. The difference is well illustrated by Knetsch (1983).

Pecuniary externalities are a product of asset specificity, which results in 'sunk costs'. Consider a public park, some distance from a population centre whose residents have exclusive use of it. Now, a second park might be proposed that is identical to the existing one, but in closer proximity to the users. If developed, the second park might generate use and benefit, but it might also cause the existing park to be used less, with a commensurate loss in the latter's value.[14] This loss in value is a pecuniary externality imposed by the new park on the old one and can be regarded as the outcome of the competitive pressures of a new enterprise on its competing rivals.

Pecuniary externalities entail a redistribution of economic rents. For most of the period since the introduction of the 1947 Town and Country Planning Acts, the focus of attention concerning the distributional aspects of land-use planning has been on pecuniary externalities arising from the granting of planning permission.

---

and to act as an informal tax on land values. Land transactions in the market now take place on the assumption that the developer will probably be required to provide some proportion of 'affordable housing' in any medium to large-scale development scheme.

[14] The decision to invest in the new park will be influenced by the existing park to the extent that people will be willing to pay an amount for the use of the new park - the measure of its economic worth - which represents their evaluation of the advantage of the new park over the old one.

However, planners are generally unable to foresee how people will respond to the introduction of a competing firm and so are unable to know what the direction – let alone the extent – of the pecuniary externality will be.[15]

The case of technological externalities is different. Knetsch (1983) quotes the example of a block of flats so sited that it interferes with the water regimen in the area and induces flooding of the ground floors of existing flats. Here the losses involved are real resource costs and are not simply a loss forced on the old flat owners by the re-evaluation of assets arising from competitive pressures. In such a case the desirability of the new project can be judged only by including the cost imposed by its impact on the neighbouring structure. Thus the total real cost of the new building to the economy includes not only the outlays for land, labour and materials necessary for construction, but also the loss inflicted upon the old building through the technological externalities involved.

Technological externalities are directly relevant to the economic efficiency with which productive resources, including land, are used. Land-use policy should therefore favour the internalisation of the costs of technological externalities (Stephen, 1987). Moreover, the economically efficient system of land-use planning is the one that internalises technological externalities at least cost.

Public Goods

Technological externalities are a species of institutional failure – they result from a failure of the current institutions (especially private law) to enable private agreements to settle disputes. Another kind of institutional failure is the failure to provide the desired quantities of environmental public goods. A public good is a good that is non-exclusive (it is not possible to prevent anyone from benefiting from it) and non-rivalrous in consumption (one person's consumption of the good does not affect another's).[16] These

---

[15] For example, the new park may draw in more visitors than it can handle, generating a positive externality for the owners of the existing park, which may benefit by altering their exclusive use rule and charging for non-residents. Alternatively, the users of the original park may benefit from the reduction in pressure upon the use of facilities such as swings and roundabouts that were previously shared by many children.

[16] The primary difference between a public good and a technological externality is that, in the case of a public good, all members of the community consume the same good,

characteristics mean that public goods will, in theory, be underprovided unless people are coerced into paying for them.[17] The classic example of a public good is defence.

The provision of certain public goods is also a legitimate function of land-use planning. Examples of activities that might be justified on these grounds are: the conservation of biological diversity, natural landscapes, and historic buildings and monuments, as well as the provision of public parks for recreation.[18]

Sustainable Development

In recent years, the problem of defining planning objectives has been complicated by the policy of promoting sustainable development, which arose from the passage of Agenda 21 at the 1992 'Earth Summit'.[19] In January 1994, the British Government published a document – *Sustainable Development: The UK Strategy* (Cm. 2426) – which examined how Agenda 21 could be implemented in the United Kingdom. This document identified the land-use planning system as a key instrument in promoting sustainable development. Virtually all planning guidance has consequently been revised, although it is by no means clear that the

---

whereas, for an externality, the good (or bad) consumed by second parties may differ from that consumed by the direct purchaser. When a person contributes to the purchase of flowers for the local Town Square, she helps to finance a public good (assuming that the whole community uses the town square and benefits in some way from the flowers). When she plants flowers in her backyard, she creates a positive externality for those neighbours who see and enjoy them (Mueller, 1989).

[17] However, see Schmidtz (1991) for a fascinating discussion of alternative mechanisms of provision.

[18] Although not all of these can be classified as pure public goods, each of them is, to some extent, necessarily a matter for public policy. For at least some of them, public policy has, in recent years, become increasingly sophisticated. For example, since the signing of the international Convention on the Conservation of Biological Diversity, considerable effort has made to develop costed targets for the conservation of the UK's habitats and species (UK Biodiversity Steering Group, 1995; Willis, Garrod and Shepherd, 1996).

[19] In 1992, in Rio de Janeiro, the United Nations held its Conference on Environment and Development (UNCED), known as the Earth Summit.The participating countries adopted a document, known as Agenda 21, which set out a programme whereby national governments would pursue policies based on the concept of sustainable development and submit regular reports on progress to a newly established United Nations Commission on Sustainable Development (UNCSD).

concept of sustainable development can bear the weight of policy development that has been placed upon it.

The concept of sustainable development was advocated and popularised by the Brundtland Report,[20] in which it was defined as 'development that meets the needs of the present without compromising the ability of future generations to meet their own needs'. The difficulty of using this definition for operational purposes was pointed out in the British Government's response to the Brundtland Report:

> 'The [Brundtland] Report defines sustainable development as meeting the needs of the present without compromising the ability of future generations to meet their own needs. There can be no quarrel with this as a general definition. The key point is how to translate it into practice, how to measure it, and to assess progress towards its achievement.' (DoE, 1988, p.13)

As a contribution towards the resolution of this conundrum, the Department of the Environment subsequently commissioned David Pearce to examine the operational content of 'sustainable development' (Corkindale, 1993). In his report, Pearce distinguished between 'strong' and 'weak' sustainability (see Pearce et al., 1989, which is a slightly amended version of this report). Strong sustainability was defined as a requirement to preserve intact the environment in all its forms as we find it today. Weak sustainability, on the other hand, allows for some natural resources to be run down as long as adequate compensation is provided by increases in other resources.[21]

More recently, Wilfred Beckerman (1995) has made a number of trenchant criticisms both of the definition of sustainable development proposed by Brundtland and of the concepts of strong and weak sustainability. Of the Brundtland definition, he says that it is totally useless since 'need' is a subjective concept. People at

---

[20] The 1987 report of the World Commission on Environment and Development, 'Our Common Future', became known as the Brundtland report after the chairman of the World Commission, Mrs Brundtland, the then Prime Minister of Norway.

[21] It was suggested that the replacement of natural by man-made capital might be consistent with sustainable development provided that the increase in man-made capital was sufficient to compensate future generations for any fall in their welfare that might have been caused by the depletion of natural capital.

different points in time, or at different income levels, or with different cultural or national backgrounds, will differ about what needs they regard as important. Hence, the injunction to enable future generations to meet their needs does not provide any clear guidance as to what has to be preserved in order that future generations may do so.

Beckerman's criticisms of the concepts of strong and weak sustainability reveal their emptiness too. He argues that such an absolutist concept of sustainable development as strong sustainability is morally repugnant; given the poverty and environmental degradation in which many of the world's population live, it is not possible to justify using up vast resources in an attempt, say, to preserve every single one of the millions of species that exist. The emptiness of the concept of weak sustainability is also exposed:

> '...if the choice between preserving natural capital and adding to (or preserving) man-made capital depends on which makes the greater contribution to welfare, the concept of sustainable development becomes redundant. In the attempt to rid the original 'strong' concept of sustainable development of its most obvious weaknesses, the baby has been thrown out with the bath water. For it appears now that what society should aim at is not 'sustainability', but the maximisation of welfare. In other words it should pursue the old fashioned economist's concept of "optimality".' (Beckerman, 1995, p.29)

Defined in terms of weak and strong sustainability, 'sustainable development' turns out to be less than useful as an objective for land-use planning purposes.[22] However, Beckerman's comments suggest that, if we are serious about our commitment to sustainable development (defined as economic optimality), then we also have to be serious about the introduction of more efficient mechanisms

---

[22] The concept of sustainability does, however, have a precise meaning in relation to the exploitation of renewable resources. Harvesting of a renewable resource beyond the maximum sustainable yield will lead to the extinction of that resource (although the optimal rate of harvesting, in the sense described by Beckerman, may be higher or lower than is implied by the maximum sustainable yield). For non-renewable resources, the concept of a maximum sustainable yield has no meaning (although such resources can, in a sense, be enhanced through the discovery of new deposits or through technological advances that make it economically feasible to recover a resource from low-grade materials).

for achieving environmental goals, such as market-based instruments, and the development of a system of land-use planning that best achieves the objective of ensuring that resources are allocated to their highest-valued use.

3. Property Rights, Economics and Planning

Public land-use planning is not the only mechanism available for internalising externalities and providing public goods. Analyses of other mechanisms have provided insights into the nature of the problem of land use and have led to the development of an economic theory of property rights that helps us to understand the rôle of the planning system. A brief discussion of these mechanisms is thus worthwhile.

The Evolution of Property Rights and the Rôle of the Common Law

Historically, the delineation of several property rights in land has often been a response to increases in population. In primitive societies, systems of land tenure that do not rely on private property in land have at least one feature in common: certain individuals or families are recognised as having cultivation rights within a given area of land whilst others are excluded from such rights. Initially, when land is plentiful, each family retains the exclusive right to the plot it has cleared and cultivated until the harvest has been reaped but it has no particular interest in (or right to) returning to the same plot. With increasing population pressure, however, good plots of cultivable land become scarce. The cultivators may then wish to begin to recultivate a given plot before the normal period of fallow has elapsed. Under such conditions, a family is likely to become more and more attached to the plot they have been cultivating on earlier occasions. Ultimately, the attachment of individual families to individual plots becomes more permanent and, by the same token, the general right of members of the tribe to clear a new plot becomes less valuable. At this point owner occupation and landlord/tenant relations become the characteristic forms of land tenure (Boserup, 1965).

More generally, it has been argued that property rights evolve in response to changes in demand and improvements in technology. In a well-known study of the Montagnois Indians of Labrador, Demsetz (1967) noted that, prior to the arrival of the Europeans, beaver habitats were held as common property, but that the opening up of the European market increased the value of beaver pelts and, in consequence, beaver habitats were converted to several property (that is to say, they became the property of individuals, rather than being owned by the group).

The courts have a key rôle to play in the delineation of property rights. In countries operating under the common law, court rulings serve as precedents for new rulings. When private disputes end in common law courts, resolution of the particular dispute ensues, and, since court rulings become precedents for similar cases, litigants are, in effect, also resolving others' disputes. As a result, the resolution of individual private disputes can be and has been a means of protecting the environment more generally (Brubaker, 1995; Morris, 1998).

Whilst precedent allows the law to achieve some measure of uniformity and provides a degree of certainty over the likely outcome of a case, the common law nevertheless remains flexible. Differing conditions can give rise to different property régimes, even at the same time and within the same common law country. Consider the two distinct legal doctrines that govern the use of water in the United States (Barzel, 1989). In the eastern states, the prevailing system, which derives from English common law, is riparian, permitting landowners reasonable use of water from rivers that run by their properties. In the western states, which are by contrast more arid and where water has a correspondingly higher value, water rights are more thoroughly delineated and the prevailing system is appropriative, granting individuals rights to water. New Mexico, the most arid of all the states, defines water in consumption terms, by reference to the net amount of water retained by the landowner. In general, the greater the scarcity of water, the greater its value, and the more it will be worth spending in terms of monitoring and enforcement, the more it will come to approximate several property. The trend towards water metering in the United Kingdom can be seen as a reaction to the apparently inexorable increase in demand for water.

The Normative Economic Theory of Property

Whilst research concerning the evolution of property rights helps us to understand why changes to property law occurred in the past, they do not necessarily help us to formulate guidelines for the evaluation of policy. For these purposes, what is needed is a set of decision rules against which government policy on the delineation and enforcement of property rights can be assessed. The starting point for this is the normative economic theory of property. Cooter and Ulen (1988) distinguish two Normative Principles of Property Law. First, the Normative Hobbes Theory: structure the law to minimise the harm caused by failures in private agreements. Second, the Normative Coase Theorem: structure the law so as to minimise the impediments to private agreements.

The Normative Hobbes theory derives from the fact that voluntary exchange is mutually beneficial but, as Hobbes argued, if people are not constrained to operate within a legal framework that encourages them to stick to agreements then they will tend to break those agreements. If the law is structured in such a way as to reduce the likelihood that agreements will be broken, the prospects for voluntary exchange are improved. Thus, the common law courts have taken a dim view of the theft of property and the breach of contract.

The Normative Coase Theory derives from the observation that voluntary bargaining was often costly because discovering an agreed solution might require extensive negotiation, whilst enforcing it might require monitoring and policing (Coase, 1960). There are many obstacles to co-operative bargaining. Negotiation, in particular, involves communication, and the costs of negotiation depend, in large part, upon the number of parties to the dispute and their geographical dispersion. Voluntary exchange is more likely to be successful when property rights are clear and less likely to be successful when property rights are ambiguous. Property law therefore favours criteria for determining ownership and property rights that are clear and simple. For example, the law gives weight to possession and use when determining ownership.

These two normative principles of property law have wide application in law and are also at the heart of the economic analysis of property rights. Their importance is illustrated by Littlechild (1978) regarding a common law judgement relating to the River Spey in Scotland. The judgement in question held that the owners of salmon fishing rights on the river do not have the right to prevent public use of the waters for canoeing and sailing. As Littlechild pointed out, this decision established a property right where the situation was not previously well defined, but the resulting property right, being held by 'the public', was not transferable. Even if the value of salmon fishing, uninterrupted by canoeing and sailing, had been higher than the value of the canoeing and sailing, it is difficult to see how potential fishermen could have bought the right to fish from potential boaters. Had the legal decision gone the other way, it would have been straightforward for potential boaters to negotiate with the easily-identified owners of fishing rights. Far from protecting the rights of the public at large, this legal decision may have prevented the use of the river's resources in the way the public would have preferred.[23]

Coase also emphasised that, where there are conflicting interests, if a decision favours one party, the other party is harmed. In doing so he subtly undermined the notion that the physical causation of harm is pertinent to decision making about technological externalities. The claim 'A hurt B' has no economic relevance. The harm results from the proximity of two incompatible activities – remove one and the harm disappears. Losses are therefore the result of two conflicting or interfering activities and are properly to be treated as the joint cost of both activities. This is also true of the expenses incurred to settle claims arising from such disputes.[24]

---

[23] Coase's analysis emphasises the importance of transaction costs as a principal determinant of the law's effect on economic activity and economic behaviour. Transaction costs can be defined as the costs of information and bargaining, and of defining, policing and enforcing property rights and contracts. Transaction costs sometimes block mutually beneficial exchange and co-operation. The judgement in the River Spey case, referred to above, had the effect of increasing transactions costs in the sense that it made it that much more difficult for competing interests to co-operate in finding a mutually acceptable solution to the problem of how to allocate access to and use of the river.

[24] Some economists have thus argued that the function of law is not to prevent all harm, but rather to balance the interests of the victim against the interests of the injurer and of the rest of society. In economic terms, this means balancing the losses due to the harm and the costs of preventing the harm. When the sum of these costs is minimised we have the 'efficient' or 'optimal' level of harm. Of course, measuring those costs and benefits is far from simple and it is not entirely clear that the law actually follows the rules that economics posits for it.

Liability Rules and Property Rules

The choice of remedy for resolving disputes about incompatible property uses – that is, in circumstances where one person is illegitimately interfering with another person's property – is an important example of the application of the normative principles of property law (Calabresi and Melamed, 1972). Where a technological externality has arisen, the courts have a choice to make between compensatory damages (making use of a liability rule) and an injunction (making use of a property rule). Where there are few obstacles to voluntary negotiation, the preferred remedy would be a property rule involving the award of an injunction against the defendant's interference with the plaintiff's property. Where there are obstacles to voluntary negotiation, the preferred remedy is a liability rule involving the award of compensatory money damages.[25]

Easements and Covenants

The Normative Coase Theory suggests that one important rôle of the legislature is to reduce transaction costs, thereby enabling more private negotiation and tort actions to take place. Easements and covenants are examples of the form of agreement to which

---

[25] The primacy of injunctive relief in England derives from the judgement of *Pride of Derby v British Celanese* [1953] Ch. 149: if A proves that his proprietary rights are being wrongly interfered with by B, and B intends to continue the wrong, then A is *prima facie* entitled to an injunction (Stephen, 1988). The preferred legal remedy depends in large part on how many parties must participate in a settlement. Where the dispute involves a small number of contiguous property owners, the costs of voluntary bargaining are likely to be low, and bargaining is likely to be successful. In these circumstances, the most efficient remedy for resolving property disputes will be injunctive relief. On the other hand, where the number of property owners is large and they are geographically dispersed, the costs of voluntary bargaining will be high and bargaining is likely to be unsuccessful. In these circumstances, the efficient legal remedy is for the courts to determine compensatory damages. In England, the circumstances under which compensation, rather than an injunction, is granted derive from *Shelfer v City of London Electric Lighting Co.* [1895] 1 Ch. 287 (Stephen, 1988). These are:

1. if the injury to the plaintiff's legal right is small; or
2. is one which is capable of being estimated in money; or
3. is one which can be adequately compensated by a small monthly payment; or
4. the case is one in which it would be oppressive to the defendant to grant an injunction.

voluntary negotiations over land use might lead. Knetsch (1983) argues in favour of a system of easements to reduce uncertainty about investment in land development. Users of land generating nuisance in the form of pollution, etc., would be required to purchase easements from neighbouring landowners, thereby internalising the externality. The neighbouring landowners would be compensated for the loss in the value of their land, and prospective purchasers of the neighbouring land wishing to use it for a purpose which required a cessation of the nuisance generating activity would have to buy back the easement.

Another possibility is the covenant which can be publicly registered as a restriction on the use of land. A party sensitive to a use to which a neighbour might put his land could purchase from the second party the latter's right to do what would otherwise be lawful. A party seeking a restrictive covenant would be likely to want it to 'run with the land', that is, to be binding on subsequent owners. Houston, Texas has been quoted as an example of how restrictive covenants can be used as an alternative to the public regulation of land use (Ellickson, 1973).

The Polluter Pays Principle

The law does not always restrict environmental externalities. For example, aesthetic nuisance is not actionable.[26] In addition, a business operating under statutory authority may be exempt from certain kinds of nuisance action. For example, a clause in the Civil Aviation Act introduced in 1922 expressly forbids legal action for reason only of noise nuisance. Government might wish to distinguish, and often does distinguish, between externalities that are a 'legitimate' source of grievance, and those that are not. The question of which externalities are to count and which not depends, in the last resort, upon a consensus in society.

Such considerations inevitably affect the judgements that planning authorities make about how far externalities generated by land developments should be internalised. One principle that might govern decision-making is the classical liberal dictum that the freedom of a man to pursue his own interest has to be qualified

---

[26] *Dalton v Anjus* (1881) 6 App. Cas 740; *Hunter v. Canary Wharf* [1997] 2 All ER 426, per Lord Goff.

insofar as it reduces the freedom of others to pursue their interest (Spencer, 1850). To paraphrase Mishan (1971), the freedom of the prospective soap manufacturer to spread smoke over the inhabitants of an area is not on all fours with the freedom of the inhabitants to continue to enjoy unpolluted air. For the mere action of the inhabitants in enjoying the unpolluted air does not of itself cause any damage to the prospective soap maker, whereas the action of the prospective soap maker – the emission of smoke into the vicinity of the inhabitants – would of itself reduce the welfare of the inhabitants. In considering a planning application for a new soap manufacturing plant, the planning authority adhering to this doctrine might be expected to base its decision on the assumption that the soap manufacturer should not be allowed to reduce the welfare of the local inhabitants in this manner. If the soap manufacturer wishes to produce in this area, he will have to pay for the harm it creates. This is the Polluter Pays Principle (PPP). Adherence to the PPP is seen as a way of ensuring that pollution externalities are internalised (D. Pearce, 1989).[27]

An extension of the PPP increasingly being discussed is the User Pays Principle (UPP), which implies that the price of a natural resource should include not only the cost of extracting or harvesting the resource, but also any extraction-associated externalities and 'user cost' elements.[28] User costs are defined as the benefits forgone by consuming a resource now rather than leaving it for future consumption (OECD, 1994b). In land-use planning, issues of user costs and extraction-associated externalities arise most obviously in relation to the extraction of non-renewable resources. The UPP also has important implications for the development of

---

[27] Although the PPP seems an unexceptionable policy principle, it is not hard to find examples of policies which fly in the face of it. One such is the Nitrate Sensitive Areas policy designed to address the problem of nitrate pollution of ground water. The cost of the policy of reducing rates of nitrate fertilizer usage in Nitrate Sensitive Areas is borne, not by the farmer or by the consumer, but by the taxpayer. Ostensibly, the reason has to do with the difficulty of applying the PPP in agriculture because of the diffuse nature of agricultural pollution, though the real reason probably has to do with the inability of farmers, given the nature of the market for agricultural produce, to pass on the costs of adherence to the PPP to the consumer.

[28] This has been put forward as an economically efficient pricing mechanism in the provision of water services (OECD, 1987). Under the UPP, subsidisation by taxpayers and cross-subsidisation among water service users would be abolished.

greenfield sites and, as we shall see, for land-use planning more generally.

4. The Privatisation of Land Development Rights

Some writers have argued that the rôle of voluntary negotiations between individual decision-makers is of limited applicability for environmental and land-use planning policy.[29] Negotiation is assumed to be precluded by the presence of a large number of individuals (either on the side that generates the externalities, or on the side that suffers from them). Consequently, it is assumed that the kind of small numbers analysis on which the Normative Coase Theory seems to depend does not apply (Baumol and Oates, 1988). As a result, most commentators hold to the view that some form of public regulation of land use is inevitable and that the costs and difficulty of achieving voluntary negotiation mean that it should be eliminated altogether. However, this view is not held universally and there are some strong arguments in favour of allowing more voluntary agreements.

The Economics of Privatisation

At present, the British land-use planning system does not accommodate, except in a very limited way, voluntary exchange between landowners and communities.[30] The absence of

---

[29] An important limitation of the use of property law and private agreements in the field of land use is that, in densely populated countries like the United Kingdom, there are often too many competing interests to make meaningful litigation possible. It is generally recognised that, where the number of individuals concerned is large, the likelihood of voluntary negotiations becomes small, because the administrative costs of co-ordination become prohibitive (Baumol and Oates, 1988). A related point is that, as the number of participants becomes critically large, the individual will more and more come to treat the behaviour of others as beyond his own possible range of influence (Buchanan, 1967).

[30] A notable exception is the concept of 'planning gain' as defined in section 52 of the 1971 Town and Country Planning Act which has now been superseded by section 106 of the 1991 Planning and Compensation Act. The latter introduced the concept of 'planning obligations'. Although couched in different language, the two are in effect the same thing, but the new Act gave broader powers to local planning authorities and symbolised a belief on the part of the then government that agreement between local authorities and land owners/ developers should be used as a means of injecting private finance into public infrastructure.

arrangements to facilitate the voluntary exchange of land development rights is an obstacle to efficient land use (Fischel, 1988). Just as the legal judgement about the use of the River Spey (above, pp. 34-35) was not conducive to efficient resource allocation in the use of that river's resources, so the nationalisation of land development rights under the terms of the 1947 Town and Country Planning Acts has not been conducive to the efficient use of land. Land-use efficiency would be improved if planning permission could be bought and sold (Mills, 1990).

An important source of inefficiency in British land-use planning is related to the lack of openness in decision-making by planning authorities. Stephen (1987) argues that the extant decision-making procedures are not conducive to the production of clear public policy goals, and that the tradition of 'ad hoc decisions in smoke-filled rooms' generates uncertainty for landowners and developers. This lack of openness is a further important argument for the privatisation of land development rights.

In an ideal world, the efficiency gains that are associated with the privatisation of state-owned industry might perhaps be achieved by leaving industry in public ownership and imposing different operational rules. However, this ignores the problem of economic calculation under centralised control: factor prices become distorted, leading to inappropriate allocation of resources (von Mises, 1921; Steele, 1992). In addition, experience shows that the state will always be tempted to shield public enterprises from competition and subsidise their inefficiency. Given the inadequacies of any actual state, privatisation is the only answer (Rowthorn and Chang, 1993). The economic argument in favour of the privatisation of land development rights is essentially similar: the state cannot be relied upon to make economically efficient decisions about development proposals, nor is it able to make satisfactory judgements about the appropriate balance between economic and environmental gains and losses.

There are, nevertheless, practical difficulties standing in the way of the privatisation of development rights. The principal ones have been articulated by Malcolm Grant in his 1988 Denman lecture.[31] If

---

[31] The Town and Country Planning Acts embody three rights. First, landowners have the right to continue to use their land and property in its existing use, together with any of

one were redesigning property rights to substitute for the existing system of regulation, the maintenance of environmental quality would require a redefinition in order to restrict lawful externalities beyond the tolerances presently actionable in nuisance or trespass. Professor Grant asserts that the courts should not be left to hammer out the necessary extensions to existing liability rules; there is a difference between gradual evolution of common law doctrine to meet changing circumstances and the need suddenly to fill a vacuum previously occupied by regulation. Just how extensive this vacuum would be has been clarified in the House of Lords judgement on *Tesco Stores plc versus Secretary of State for the Environment* (House of Lords, May 1995). In that judgement, all responsibility for the task of establishing the proper relationship between the conditions for planning permission and the projected impact of the proposed development was abdicated (Grant, 1995).[32]

Externalities in land use and development entail conflicts of interest between the damaged and damaging parties. As has been argued above, the resolution of these conflicts should be the principal task of land-use planning. Professor Grant is obviously right to be concerned to resist policy proposals that might have the effect of reducing or removing a landowner's defence against developments which might have an adverse impact on his own property. However, given that this defence currently consists only of the right to make representations in relation to planning

---

the permitted or exempted development rights created by the Acts and the subordinate legislation. Second, there is the right of the owner to have any application for planning permission determined by the LPA (and, on appeal, by the relevant government minister) in accordance with the law, having regard to planning and all other material considerations. This right is enforceable by application to the High Court. Third, there is the right to make representations in relation to planning applications made by others for developments which may have an adverse impact upon one's own property. This is the landowner's principal defence against otherwise non-actionable externalities.

[32] There are other relevant property rights not mentioned in Professor Grant's Denman lecture, not least the right of action in nuisance. The most harmful externalities can be attacked through a nuisance action, but, in the absence of statutory guidance, the courts have often struggled with the problem of identifying what is a nuisance. Recurring questions have been, for example, whether 'coming to a nuisance' should be any defence (on which the courts of the UK and the USA have taken diametrically opposed stances); and whether activities constituting a nuisance in one area should be held to be capable of constituting a nuisance in another area, even if there are important economic, environmental and social differences between the two.

applications made by others, there is surely a need to move in the opposite direction and to strengthen such a person's ability to defend his own interests. Not only should individuals be able to make representations about the nature and extent of the externalities that they anticipate will be associated with any development, but they should also be able to pursue such representations in the courts.

One way to achieve this would be to apply the User Pays Principle in land-use planning. To do this, it would be necessary for government to define, in law, what constitutes an acceptable, and what an unacceptable, externality for land-use planning purposes. Thus, the developer would be required to conform to a set of minimum environmental quality standards (these might for example include restrictions on the height of buildings and/or the noise level at the perimeter of the development).[33] Under such a régime, there would be a presumption that the landowner had the right to develop his land provided that he conformed to the standards. Those in the vicinity of a development would have standing to challenge it in the courts if they could show that it might breach the applicable standards.[34] It would then be for the courts to decide whether the development was in fact in breach and, if so, whether it should be enjoined or whether the community should be granted additional compensation.

Land-Use Planning in Ontario

The superiority of such a land-use planning régime has been illustrated in a comparative study of the systems of development control in Great Britain and in the Canadian Province of Ontario (Stephen, 1987). In considering planning appeals, the British courts adopt what is essentially a property rule in their approach to disputes about planning permission. The development is either allowed or it is prevented. Where a planning authority has, in the court's view, behaved unreasonably or imposed a condition that fails its tests, the matter is returned to the planning authority for

---

[33] These could be set locally, with proposed restrictions being put to a referendum, or set by an elected planning board.

[34] Environmental organisations might sponsor such actions by agreeing to indemnify plaintiffs.

further consideration. The courts have seldom severed a condition they have considered unlawful from a grant of planning permission. Quashing a condition of any significance usually means that the whole decision is quashed. The LPA's right to make a planning decision is not abrogated. Where their decision to grant planning permission subject to conditions is quashed, the planning authority might simply decide to refuse planning permission altogether. It is up to the parties – developer and LPA – to bargain around that entitlement, but the consent of the LPA must be obtained before development takes place.

In Ontario, by contrast, developers compensate the Ontario Municipal Board (who are the local planning authority) for the external costs associated with the development. The Ontario system has a feature that enables the municipality to defend its entitlement to control development: a judicially determined price (or impact fee) at which the entitlement is transferred. However, the damages are determined *ex ante* with the grant of permission. The system thus incorporates aspects of both a property rule (non-conforming uses are enjoined) and a liability rule (damages are paid to the community for uses that, whilst conforming to the rules, nevertheless impose external costs on the community).

A key difference between the British and Ontario land-use planning systems is in the use made of planning agreements. In Great Britain, the principal mechanism available to LPAs for the purpose of internalising externalities is 'planning gain'. Section 52 of the 1971 Town and Country Planning Act provides that an LPA may enter into an agreement with a developer 'for a purpose of restricting or regulating the development or use of land, either permanently or during such period as may be prescribed by the agreement'.[35] The principal benefit to be gained by the LPA through planning by agreement is that it permits the local authority to obtain material benefits or control aspects of development which, if attempted by attaching conditions to a grant of planning permission, would be *ultra vires* (Stephen, 1988).

A criticism that can be levelled at planning gain as it currently operates in Great Britain is that the LPAs have a monopoly over the

---

[35] This section has now been superseded by section 106 of the 1991 Planning and Compensation Act, although the content of that clause is similar.

allocation of local development rights and have discretion to determine what developments are permissible on a case-by-case basis. LPAs are thus in a position to exploit their monopoly position to extract unreasonable concessions from developers. As a result, the system is likely to be inefficient, especially if developers have to go through costly negotiations with the LPA before their application is permitted, but also where negotiations are not open and there is a lack of information which may cause markets to work inefficiently, and where concessions from the developer to the local authority intended to compensate residents for any disamenity suffered are not directed to those most adversely affected. In granting planning permissions, LPAs in Great Britain are able to impose conditions on developers, which require them to rectify the adverse effects of their proposed developments. In Ontario, on the other hand, the Municipal Board has sought to define the terms of such agreements by making them compensatory in nature and subject to judicial review.

The User Pays Principle in Land-Use Planning

In his Denman lecture, Professor Grant concluded that, whilst economists were right to charge the planning system with being expensive, economically unaccountable and paternalistically self-satisfied, planners were entitled to defend themselves by arguing that removing the planning system would result in a legal vacuum and that it remained to be seen whether alternative economic approaches would succeed as well in providing environmental protection with economic efficiency (Grant, 1988). It has been argued here that the legal vacuum could be filled by the application of the User Pays Principle in land-use planning including the adoption of compensatory arrangements in lieu of environmental externalities, possibly along the lines of the Ontario model.

The definition of land-use quality standards would introduce greater openness and reduce or remove the element of administrative discretion in British land-use planning. It would also open the way to the possibility of a more flexible approach to planning agreements between developers and planning authorities, whereby planning permission could be bought and sold at a price calculated to compensate for the costs of the environmental externalities imposed by land developments on the rest of the community. In effect, the User Pays Principle would be applied to constrain the right to develop land.

Perhaps the most difficult question to be addressed in implementing this proposal is how the local planning authority determines the external costs.[36] Official efforts to improve the measurement of externalities in land-use planning are currently being driven by European legislation, notably Directive 85/337/EEC, which requires the preparation of environmental statements for various categories of development project.[37] Environmental statements are theoretically capable of yielding important information about the nature and extent of environmental externalities likely to be associated with development projects, and thus of improving decision-making about planning applications. Their use was advocated in reports commissioned by the Department of the Environment (Land Use Consultants, 1994a, b), which suggested that, in considering potential environmental impacts, the planning authority needs to address two basic questions. The first concerns the relationships between the different kinds of environmental impact and the relative weight to be attached to each of them. The second concerns the way the economic, social and environmental factors are to be drawn together in reaching the final decision on the planning application. The reports also point out that planning authorities should not be so much concerned with the question of whether or not a privately sponsored development will be profitable or financially viable. Planning authorities should, rather, be concerned about the wider costs and benefits of any scheme, such as whether the environmental costs of the proposed development will be offset by external environmental or other benefits, and whether conditions might be imposed on the developer that would improve the chances of a net environmental/social benefit being obtained.

---

[36] Environmental assessment and valuation has been advocated by the DoE (DoE, 1991) and the problems associated with applying such techniques in the field of land-use planning are increasingly being discussed in academic circles (Lichfield, 1996; Schofield, 1987).

[37] The EC Directive has been given effect in England and Wales under the terms of the 1988 Town and Country Planning (Assessment of Environmental Effects) Regulations.

It is, of course, difficult to resolve such questions in the absence of information about the subjective preferences of the local people who would be affected by the development (and who are the primary ostensible beneficiaries of the planning system). One way to get around this problem would be simply to auction development rights. If the bid from a conservation organisation were higher than that submitted by a developer, then the land would be conserved; otherwise it would be developed. There is evidence that were the existing land-use planning legislation replaced with such an auction system, a combination of for-profit and not-for-profit conservation schemes would step into the breach, both rectifying degraded sites and conserving desirable sites (Pennington, 1996). Nevertheless, some communities may prefer not to have certain kinds of development on their doorstop at all. The problem is to know what kinds are desired and what not. Thus, an essential component of reform of the land-use planning system would be to give local people more voice in the affairs of their community, for example by having an elected planning committee. Planners would stand for election on a platform of a particular set of planning principles.[38] Such a system would have much in common with a system of zoning, which is discussed in the next section.

---

[38] Most likely some planners would advertise their conservationist ethic, whilst others would advertise the benefits of allowing more development, perhaps stressing the reduction in local taxes that could result from large bids for development.

5. Zoning and Tradable Development Rights

Land use zoning is another way in which the problem of internalising environmental externalities can be addressed. Zoning is the dominant form of planning in Canada, the USA and elsewhere outside the United Kingdom (Cullingworth and Nadin, 1994).[39] The principle of zoning in the USA is that a local government divides its area into zones on a map and sets regulations prescribing permissible uses of land and limitations on the physical shape of new development.

During the 1980s, the UK Government introduced Simplified Planning Zones, which enable planning authorities to specify in advance the types of development that are acceptable in an area, thus removing the uncertainty and delay perceived as inherent in the prevailing discretionary system of planning control.

The relative importance that people attach to the environment and to development varies from place to place. What constitutes an

---

[39] The comparison of land-use planning experience in the UK and the USA has been the subject of a study by Wakeford (1990) who concluded that 'the British system starts with discretion and imports some certainty (but no Guarantees) by ensuring that the development plan influences decisions, and by providing an appeal process to help achieve consistency of decisions', whereas, in the USA, 'land use zoning started by designating precisely what could be done on land - certainty if ever there was any'. However, there are many different variants upon the US system in the USA and elsewhere which range from, at one extreme, a situation which is virtually indistinguishable from the British planning system, in which a discretionary consent is required from one or more public agencies before development can be carried out; to jurisdictions in which the zoning scheme may be very basic, and will establish the limits to the development rights of landowners and require no further consent for development which remains within those limits. It is therefore misleading to think of the US arrangements as if they were one homogeneous system: they are not. The certainty that zoning is often thought to provide is in fact often illusory. Although the zoning map and ordinance establish the entitlements, it is always possible for them to be subject to a variance. Many major land use battles in the USA are fought on the basis of variances, rather than on the initial ordinances themselves. Moreover, because the ordinances are, in some jurisdictions, frequently amended, the property rights that they confer change over time. In the UK, the property right is conferred by grant of planning permission; in the USA, it is by the zoning. However, once the property right is established in the British system, it endures, provided the permission is implemented within the specified time (normally five years). In the USA, it can be withdrawn, even at a relatively late stage.

important environmental externality in an area of great natural beauty might be regarded as an insignificant matter in an area recently blighted by the demise of the dominant local industry.[40] Simplified Planning Zones, as well as Enterprise Zones with relatively weak development constraints, were introduced in areas of 'social and economic deprivation' and they consequently focused more on how to facilitate development than on how to conserve the environment (Arup Economic Consultants, 1991). However, there is no reason why the concept should not be applied more generally, even in environmentally sensitive areas. The emphasis of the planning rules in such areas would of course be different, with a presumption that the negative environmental externalities arising from prospective developments should be more severely restricted.

In addition to locational differences, preferences vary over time. Thus the appropriate zoning régime should be sufficiently flexible to allow periodic amendments. In principle, there could be regular local referenda (say, every five years) on the type of zone in which people want to live.

Economic Evaluation of Zoning

Economic evaluation enables a better understanding of land use zoning systems and provides guidance as to what kind of system might function best. In general, the appropriate decision criterion against which a system of zoning proposals should be evaluated is whether it is likely to reduce the extent of the negative externalities to which people are exposed by an amount greater than the costs associated with implementing and enforcing it (Pogodzinski and Sass, 1990).[41] A comprehensive review of this subject is beyond

---

[40] Research by Murdoch et al. (1992) suggests that the approach to minerals planning varies considerably from one part of the country to another primarily because of differences in local preferences. Thus, while some of the residents of Buckinghamshire (with the support of conservation bodies such as the Council for the Protection of Rural England) sought to displace extraction activity to other areas, the residents of Cumbria and Devon (and other regions such as the Highlands of Scotland) were less vocal, suggesting that they are more prepared to live with minerals workings, presumably because of the associated economic benefits.

[41] This is easier said than done. In their review of the economics of zoning, Pogodzinski and Sass (1990) examined research on the following subjects:

the scope of this paper. However, there are various practical objections to zoning (Harrison, 1977).

First, any zoning system will have implications for transport costs. In principle, it is possible to design a layout of houses, employment and transport which minimises journey-to-work transport costs. The difference in transport costs between this layout and the transport costs under a zoning solution would be a measure of the cost at which the benefits of freedom from environmental nuisance were being bought. In practice, however, such an analysis is impossible, since employment practices vary over time and planners are not able to prevent people from moving between zones; so what may seem an ideal zoning system in theory may turn out to be the very worst one in practice. Can the planners have foreseen that by restricting development in the Green Belt around London, Chelmsford and Guildford would more rapidly become commuter towns?

Second, by its very nature, zoning does not allow for the possibility that, although (say) an industrial zone might have been chosen carefully by the development planners, some businesses might nevertheless prefer an alternative location. For a variety of reasons, including availability of labour, ease of access to transport depots, and so on, businesses might be prepared to pay a greater sum than their rent on the industrial site for an alternative location. If they located elsewhere, they would, of course, give rise to environmental externalities. But, if the benefits to the business exceeded the extent of these external costs, the best solution might be one in which the business located outside the industrial zone and

---

1. how zoning affects the supply of housing and the land market;

2. the impact of zoning on consumer choice in the housing market;

3. Tiebout effects resulting from housing mobility in response to zoning (Tiebout, 1956);

4. externality effects associated with production externalities, agglomeration economies, externalities associated with non-conforming uses, public goods, and congestion externalities;

5. attempts to explain the economic forces giving rise to particular zoning regulations;

6. rent-seeking behaviour (Tullock, 1967; Krueger, 1974) involving the expenditure of resources by individuals to maintain or secure zoning in their own self-interest.

reduced the environmental impact either by modifying its production methods or by compensating those adversely affected.

A further group of problems concerns the costs of dealing with non-conforming uses. Whilst areas may be zoned for residential or commercial uses and future developments limited to these purposes, the zones concerned may at present contain other sorts of uses which are considered unsuitable. A policy of moving such non-conforming uses may produce benefits, but it may also impose costs. If businesses are forced to move, they may be faced with costs, such as higher rents, which they have to meet themselves; their change of location may give rise to extra costs for customers who have to travel further to obtain similar services; and such movement may lead to longer journeys to work and possibly losses of jobs for local people.

Perhaps all this suggests that zoning has generally focused on the wrong issue, namely type of use rather than the consequences of use. Few people want to live next to a factory belching out black smoke from low-rise chimneys, but how many would similarly object to living next to a factory producing microprocessors in ultra-quiet robot-controlled production lines with no emissions to air, water or land? A more sensible system of zoning might focus on the actual externalities generated by any particular land use, rather than the use itself. In addition, it seems reasonable to propose that if zoning were to be introduced then it should be done in such a way as to maximise flexibility. A means of achieving this is to allow transfer of development rights, which are discussed below (pp. 53-54).

Market-Based Instruments

It is now generally accepted that market-based instruments (MBIs), such as pollution charges and tradable permits, can help to reduce the problem of externalities (DOE, 1993; OECD, 1994a). Various advantages are claimed for market-based instruments, including:

- MBIs provide a means of achieving environmental objectives at a lower resource cost than conventional 'command-and-control' style regulations;

- MBIs provide a continuing financial incentive for producers, their suppliers and their customers to introduce innovative methods of controlling pollution in more cost-effective ways;

- MBIs allow a more flexible response to changing economic circumstances, since existing producers can expand their output and new producers can establish themselves, provided they are prepared to pay for the use they make of the environment;

- much of the information about the costs of, and technological choices about, pollution abatement reside with individual businesses. MBIs effectively devolve the use of information and reduce the likelihood of 'regulatory capture';

- some MBIs raise revenue which can be used to reduce taxation or to finance additional public expenditure.

Tradable Permits v. Emission Charges

If the social costs and benefits of an activity (say, ambient air pollution emanating from a group of factories) were known, then it would be irrelevant whether the activity were regulated using emission charges or auctioned tradable permits: the impact both in terms of overall emissions and in terms of revenue would be identical. However, we live in a world of imperfect information. In such a world, the choice between tradable permits and emission charges depends on the relative importance attached, on the one hand, to the environmental impacts and, on the other, to cost considerations. Emission charges give more certainty about the marginal cost of abatement, since producers will not spend more on abatement than they would have to pay in charges. However, they give less certainty about the precise outcome for the environment. Tradable permits, on the other hand, give more certainty about the environmental outcome, but less about the marginal cost of abatement. If there is a binding environmental constraint, a tradable permits scheme is more likely to be appropriate, whereas if the cost of meeting an environmental objective is the major concern, an emission charge may be preferred (Weitzman, 1974; Adar and Griffin, 1976).[42]

Tradable Development Rights

A MBI which has the potential to introduce an element of flexibility into zoning, in a manner analogous to the tradable permit in the field of pollution control, is the tradable development right (TDR). Under a system of TDRs, some areas might be specified as 'conservation zones' and others as 'development zones' (of course, this example is illustrative rather than exhaustive – it does not capture the full range of possibilities of the TDR system, which might include all manner of zonal characteristics). Landowners whose properties lie within conservation zones are then allocated certain 'development rights' and future development can only be carried out through the exercise of these rights. Landowners holding development rights can either exercise those rights in development zones or sell them to others. Because development rights are created only through permanent land conservation, pressure to develop also stimulates an incentive to conserve. The TDR system allows development in designated growth areas at higher density than would otherwise be allowed. The designation of conservation zones and development zones gives land users a measure of certainty, and can offer far more predictable planning and development than conventional land-use planning systems (Clark and Downes, 1995). It also offers a potentially cost-effective way of providing public conservation goods.

One of the best known examples of TDRs used for land-use planning purposes is the New Jersey Pinelands in the USA. Following the creation of the Pinelands National Reserve in 1978, the Pinelands were divided into different land zones. The most ecologically sensitive were classified as Preservation Areas. Most residential, commercial and industrial development is prohibited in Preservation Areas, although some activities, such as forestry, recreation, etc., are allowed if done in conformity with specified environmental standards. Growth is encouraged in Forest Areas, Agricultural Production Areas, Regional Growth Areas, and Rural

---

[42] For a general discussion of the practical rôle of different economic instruments in urban containment, see Clough (1996).

Development Areas, subject to environmental and zoning standards. Each of these types of area has a predetermined housing density allowance.

Development is regulated through the Pinelands Development Plan, which incorporates a system of TDRs, with transfer facilitated by a Credit Bank. The TDRs are allocated to landowners in the Preservation Areas and Agricultural Production Areas. Developers in Regional Growth Areas can then purchase them in order to increase construction density. (Rural Development Areas are treated as transition zones, in which modest development is allowed in order to reduce development pressure on Regional Growth Areas.) Landowners in preservation areas selling development credits retain title to their land and may continue to use it for authorised, non-residential uses. Prior to sale of credits, however, they must record a deed restriction binding all subsequent owners of that property to the same authorised uses (Clark and Downes, 1995).

The Habitat Transaction Method

The Habitat Transaction Method (HTM) is a variation on the TDR approach. Like TDRs, the HTM requires advance planning to preserve valuable habitat through the use of development rights. However, the HTM classifies land according to its relative habitat value, which is based on ecological criteria such as the presence of endangered species. The HTM is being applied in the Habitat Conservation Plan (HCP) developed for Kern County, California. The plan establishes a red zone of critical habitat (worth three habitat credits per acre), a green zone of moderately valuable habitat (worth two credits per acre), and a white zone of minimal habitat value where development costs one credit per acre but where there is no credit for conservation. All development is subject to a 3:1 mitigation ratio. Thus, if developers wish to build in a red zone of critical habitat, they must create nine conservation credits per acre, whereas development in a white zone of minimal habitat value requires only three credits per acre.

Unlike TDRs, HTMs do not directly restrict development on any specific piece of land. TDRs generally involve the classification of particular land areas either as 'sending' (preservation) areas or as 'receiving' (higher density) areas. In contrast, under the HTM system, every piece of land could theoretically be developed or preserved. Whilst the economic incentives steer development away from ecologically valuable habitat, there is less guarantee that critical areas will be conserved. This problem is being addressed in Kern County by introducing upper limits on the extent of development in the red zone (Clark and Downes, 1995).

Tradable Development Rights in the United Kingdom?

As has already been noted, development rights in the United Kingdom were effectively nationalised under the 1947 Town and Country Planning Acts and have subsequently been partially reallocated to certain private interests on a discretionary basis. TDRs offer a superior means of re-privatising development rights. Of course, the existing planning system would have to be scrapped, but it would not be replaced by a vacuum. Indeed, there is good reason to believe that the space left would be better occupied by a system of TDRs, since such a system would be more likely to accord to the wishes of the local people and would be more responsive to changing economic circumstances.

In addition, the introduction of a TDR system in the UK would help to break down the divisive and unhelpful perception, dating back at least to Abercrombie (1933), that a rigid distinction between the urban and the rural should be maintained. The Industrial Revolution caused millions of people to move to urban areas, taking them away from daily contact with natural scenery and wildlife. Today, over 80 per cent of the British population lives in towns and cities. Many of them do not easily gain access to the countryside or even to the urban fringe. It is arguably more important, therefore, to ensure that there is more natural green space in our cities than to preserve forever belts of greenery on their borders (Emery, 1986).

6. Conclusion: Time to Privatise Land-Development Rights

The conventional wisdom in land-use planning circles is that the 1947 Town and Country Planning Acts represent the most important step forward in the history of British land-use planning. This is not a view that is based on systematic evaluation and, as has been argued in this paper, there are good reasons for believing it to be misplaced. The problems with the land-use planning system are analogous to those previously experienced with a number of the nationalised industries. Just as many of those industries failed to deliver economic efficiency – or, often, even a service to customers – so nationalised land development rights and the large element of administrative discretion in land-use planning do not seem to be delivering results in a way that is either cost-effective or in line with what people actually want.

The British government is committed to the principle of introducing market-based instruments for environmental protection as an economically efficient way of delivering environmental policy objectives. Progress towards this goal has, however, been slow. In part, this is because the necessary research and analysis that is a precondition of such a policy change has not yet been done. In part, it is because of political opposition from vested interests and inertia in the bureaucratic system. Similar problems will have to be addressed and overcome before market-based instruments, such as an auction system or a system of zoning combined with tradable development rights, can be introduced successfully in the field of land-use planning.

The introduction of market-based instruments in land-use planning implies the possibility of voluntary exchange of land development rights. One of the most serious obstacles to such voluntary exchange is the extent of administrative discretion inherent in the current system, which is a consequence of the nationalisation of land development rights that resulted from the 1947 Acts. Although the 1990 Planning and Compensation Act seems to have reduced the extent of this discretion, there is no doubt that further primary legislation to redefine property rights would be necessary in order to pave the way for the introduction of market-based instruments.

To recapitulate: since 1947, the land-use planning system has had an inhibiting effect on the operation of the market in land and property because of the severe limitations on the voluntary exchange of property rights that have been associated with it. If this were the only way to secure the achievement of land-use planning objectives, the continuation of this system might conceivably be justified. But this is far from the case. The land-use planning objectives as currently formulated make little sense, and even if they did, there are market-based instruments available which could achieve them more efficiently. After 50 years of the Town and Country Planning Acts, it is now time to privatise land development rights.

References

Abercrombie, P. (1933): *Town and Country Planning*, London: Butterworth.

Abercrombie, P. (1944): *Greater London Plan*, London: HMSO.

Adar, Z. and Griffin, J. M. (1976): 'Uncertainty and the Choice of Pollution Control Instruments', *Journal of Environmental Economics and Management*, Vol. 3, pp. 178-88.

Arup Economic Consultants (1991): 'Simplified Planning Zones: Progress and Procedures', Department of the Environment Planning Research Programme, London: HMSO.

Barzel, Y. (1989): *Economic Analysis of Property Rights*, Cambridge: Cambridge University Press.

Baumol, W. J. and Oates, W. E. (1988): *The Theory of Environmental Policy*, Second Edition, Cambridge: Cambridge University Press.

Beckerman, W. (1995): *Small is Stupid: Blowing the Whistle on the Greens*, Duckworth.

Boserup, E. (1965): *The Conditions of Agricultural Growth: The Economics of Agrarian Change under Population Pressure*, London: George Allen and Unwin.

Bramley, G. and Watkins, S. (1996): *Steering the Housing Market: New Building and the Changing Planning System*, London: The Policy Press.

Brown, A. J. (1972): *The Framework of Regional Economics in the United Kingdom*, Cambridge: Cambridge University Press.

Brubaker, E. (1995): *Property Rights in Defence of Nature*, Toronto: Environment Probe.

Buchanan, J. M. (1967): 'Cooperation and Conflict in Public-Goods Interaction', *Western Economic Journal*, Vol. 5, pp. 109-21.

Calabresi, G. and Melamed, A. D. (1972): 'Property Rules, Liability Rules and Inalienability: One View of the Cathedral', *Harvard Law Review*, Vol. 85 (6), pp. 1,089 – 1,128.

Cheshire, P. and Sheppard, S. (1989): 'British Planning Policy and Access to the Housing Market: Some Empirical Estimates', *Urban Studies*, Vol. 26, No. 5, pp.469 – 85.

— (1996): 'Some Economic Consequences of Land-use Planning', paper presented to the 1996 AREUEA International Real Estate Conference, Orlando, Florida.

Clark, D. and Downes, D. (1995): *What Price Biodiversity? Economic Incentives and Biodiversity Conservation in the United States*, Washington DC: Center for International Environmental Law.

Clough, P. (1996): *Planning and Sustainable Management - A Re-examination of the Peri-urban Problem*, Wellington, New Zealand: New Zealand Institute of Economic Research.

Coase, R. H. (1960): 'The Problem of Social Cost', *Journal of Law and Economics*, Vol. 3 (1), pp. 1-44.

Committee on Land Utilisation in Rural Areas (1941*)*: *Final Report* (Scott Report), Cmnd. 6378, London: HMSO.

Committee on New Towns (1942): Final Report (Reith Report), Cmnd. 6876, London: HMSO.

Cooter, R. and Ulen, T. (1988): *Law and Economics*, London: Harper Collins.

Corkindale, J. T. (1993): 'Recent Developments in Environmental Appraisal', *Journal of Environmental Planning and Management*, Vol. 36, No. 1, pp. 15 – 22.

Cullingworth, J. B. and Nadin, V. (1994): *Town and Country Planning in Britain*, Eleventh Edition, London: Routledge.

Demsetz, H. (1967): 'Towards a Theory of Property Rights', *American Economic Review*, Vol. 157, pp. 347 – 59.

DOE (1988): *A Perspective by the United Kingdom on the Report of the World Commission on Environment and Development*, London: Department of the Environment.

DOE (1993): *Making Markets Work for the Environment*, London: HMSO.

DOE (1997): *Planning Policy Guidance: General Policy and Principles, PPG1 (Revised)*, London: HMSO.

DOE (1988): *The Green Belts*, London: HMSO.

DOE/Welsh Office (1992): *Planning Policy Guidance: General Policy and Principles, PPG 1*, London: HMSO.

DOE/Welsh Office (1992): *Planning Policy Guidance: The Countryside and the Rural Economy, PPG 7*, London: HMSO.

Department of Land Economy, University of Cambridge (1995): 'Developing Indicators and Measures for Evaluating the Effectiveness of Land-use Planning', Stage 1 Interim Report, unpublished.

Ellickson, R. C. (1973): 'Alternatives to Zoning: Covenants, Nuisance Rules and Fines as Land Use Controls', *University of Chicago Law Review*, Vol. 40 (4), pp. 681 – 781.

Emery, M. (1986): *Promoting Nature in Cities and Towns*, London: Croom Helm.

Evans, A. W. (1988): *No Room! No Room! The Costs of the British Town and Country Planning System*, IEA Occasional Paper No. 79, London: Institute of Economic Affairs.

— (1985): *Urban Economics: An Introduction*, Oxford: Blackwell.

Eve, G. (1992): *The Relationship between House Prices and Land Supply*, London: HMSO.

Fischel, W. A. (1985): *The Economics of the Zoning Laws: A Property Rights Approach to American Land Use Controls*, Johns Hopkins University Press.

Gordon, P. and Richardson, H. W. (1995): *The Case for Suburban and Against Compact Development*, unpublished paper.

Grant, M. (1988): 'Forty Years of Planning Control: The Case for the Defence', The Denman Lecture, Department of Land Economy, University of Cambridge.

Grant, M. (1995): 'If Tigard were an English City: Exactions Law in England following the Tesco Case', unpublished paper.

Hall, P., Gracey, H., Drewett, R., and Thomas, R. (1973): *The Containment of Urban England*, London: George Allen and Unwin.

Harrison, A. J. (1977): *Economics and Land-use Planning*, London: Croom Helm.

H M Government (1996): *Household Growth: Where shall we Live?*, Cm. 3471, London: HMSO.

H M Government (1990): *This Common Inheritance*, Cmnd. 1200, London: HMSO.

H M Government (1994): *The UK Sustainable Development Strategy*, Cm. 2426, London: HMSO.

Hobbes, T. (1651): *Leviathan*.

Howard, E. (1898): *Tomorrow: A Peaceful Path to Real Reform*, London: Swan Sonnenschein.

Knetsch, J. L. (1983): *Property Rights and Compensation: Compulsory Acquisition and Other Losses*, Canada: Butterworth.

Kreuger, A. O. (1974): 'The Political Economy of the Rent Seeking Society', *American Economic Review*, Vol. 64 (3), pp. 291 – 303.

Land Use Consultants (1994a): *Evaluation of Environmental Information for Planning Projects: A Good Practice Guide*, Department of the Environment Planning Research Programme, London: HMSO.

Land Use Consultants (1994b): *Good Practice on the Evaluation of Environmental Information for Planning Projects: The Research Report*, Department of the Environment Planning Research Programme, London: HMSO.

Lichfield, N. (1996): *Community Impact Evaluation*, London: UCL Press.

Littlechild, S. C. (1978): *The Fallacy of the Mixed Economy: An Austrian Critique of Economic Thinking and Policy*, Hobart Paper 80, London: Institute of Economic Affairs.

Mills, D. E. (1990): 'Zoning Rights and Development Timing', *Land Economics*, Vol. 64 (3).

Mishan, E. J. (1971): *Cost-Benefit Analysis: An Informal Introduction*, Second Edition, London: Unwin Hyman.

Mises, L. von (1949): *Human Action*, New Haven: Yale University Press.

Mueller, D. C. (1989): *Public Choice II*, Cambridge: Cambridge University Press.

Murdoch, J., Flynn, A. and Marsden, T. (1992): 'Uneven Regulation and the Development Process: A Comparative Analysis of Minerals Planning in Three English Regions', ESRC Countryside Change Initiative Working Paper 35, University of Newcastle-upon-Tyne.

OECD (1994): *Managing the Environment: The Rôle of Economic Instruments*, Paris: Organisation for Economic Co-operation and Development.

OECD (1987): *Pricing of Water Services*, Paris: Organisation for Economic Co-operation and Development.

OECD (1994): *Project and Policy Appraisal: Integrating Economics and Environment*, Paris: Organisation for Economic Co-operation and Development.

Pearce, B. J. (1992): 'The Effectiveness of the British Land-use Planning System', *Town Planning Review*, No. 63, Vol. 1.

Pearce, D. W. (1989): *The Polluter Pays Principle*, London Environmental Economics Centre Gatekeeper Series 89-03, London: International Institute for Environment and Development.

Pearce, D. W., Markandya, A. and Barbier, E. (1989): *Blueprint for a Green Economy*, London: Earthscan.

Pennington, M. (1996): *Conservation and the Countryside: By Quango or Market?*, IEA Studies on the Environment No. 6, London: Institute of Economic Affairs.

PIEDA (1992): *Evaluating the Effectiveness of Land-use Planning*, Department of the Environment Planning Research Programme, London: HMSO.

Pogodzinski, J. M. and Sass, T. R. (1990): 'The Economic Theory of Zoning: A Critical Review', *Land Economics*, Vol. 66 (3).

Reade, E. (1987): *British Town and Country Planning*, Open University Press.

Robbins, L. (1932): *The Nature and Significance of Economic Science*, London: Macmillan.

Rowthorn, B. and Chang, H. (1993): 'Public Ownership and the Theory of the State', in Clarke, T. and Pitalis, C. (eds.): *The Political Economy of Privatisation*, London: Routledge.

Royal Commission on the Distribution of Industrial Population (1940): *Report* (Barlow Report), Cmnd. 6153, London: HMSO.

Salter, W. E. G. (1963): *Productivity and Technical Change*, Cambridge University Press.

Schmidtz, D. (1991) *The Limits of Government – An Essay on the Public Goods Argument*, Boulder: Westview Press.

Schofield, J. A. (1987): *Cost-benefit Analysis in Urban and Regional Planning*, London: Unwin Hyman.

Spencer, H. (1850): *Social Statics*, New York: Robert Schalkenbach Foundation, 1954.

Steele, D. R. (1992): *From Marx to Mises*, La Salle: Open Court.

Stephen, F. H. (1987): 'Property Rules and Liability Rules in the Regulation of Land Development: An Analysis of Development Control in Great Britain and Ontario', *International Review of Law and Economics*, Vol. 7, pp. 33 – 49.

Stephen, F. H. (1988): *The Economics of the Law*, London: Wheatsheaf Books.

The UK Biodiversity Steering Group (1995): *Report, Vol. 1, Meeting the Rio Challenge*, London: HMSO.

Tiebout, C. M. (1956): 'A Pure Theory of Local Expenditures', *Journal of Political Economy*, Vol. 64, pp. 145 – 59.

Tullock, G. (1967): 'The Welfare Costs of Tariffs, Monopolies and Theft', *Western Economic Journal*, Vol. 5, pp. 224 – 32.

Viner, J. (1931): 'Cost Curves and Supply Curves' reprinted in Stigler, G. J. and Boulding, K. E. (eds.) (1952): *Readings in Price Theory*, Chicago: American Economic Association.

Wakeford, R. (1990): *American Development Control: Parallels from an English Perspective*, London: HMSO.

Weitzman, M. L. (1974): 'Prices vs. Quantities', *The Review of Economic Studies*, Vol. 41, pp. 477 – 90.

Willis, K. G. (1980): *The Economics of Town and Country Planning*, London: Granada.

— , Garrod, G. and Shepherd, P. (1996): *Towards a Methodology for Costing Targets and Priorities for Biodiversity Conservation in the UK*, London: HMSO.

World Commission on Environment and Development (1987): *Our Common Future* (The Brundtland Report), Oxford University Press.

Wragg, R. and Robertson, J. (1978): *Post-War Trends in Employment, Productivity, Output, Labour Costs and Prices by Industry in the United Kingdom*, Department of Employment Research Paper No. 3.

Glossary

APPRAISAL The process of defining and examining options, and of weighing costs and benefits before a decision is made.

COVENANT A restriction on the use of property inserted into the deeds.

EASEMENT The legal right to use something (especially land and property) not one's own or to prevent its owner making an inconvenient use of it.

ECONOMIC RENT The difference between what the factors, or productive services, of a resource owner can earn in their current use and the minimum sum he is prepared to accept to keep them there.

ENDOGENOUS ZONING Endogenous zoning studies attempt to explain why particular zoning regulations arise rather than treating zoning as being determined exogenously.

EVALUATION The ex-post assessment of a policy, programme or project.

EXTERNALITY An externality arises when an economic agent imposes costs or confers benefits on the rest of society which do not appear in the agent's profit and loss account.

HABITAT TRANSACTION METHOD This is a variation of Tradable Development Rights. It is similar in that it requires advance planning by a community to preserve valuable habitat through the use of development rights. However, the HTM classifies property according to its relative habitat value, which is based on ecological criteria such as the presence of endangered species.

INJUNCTION A form of equitable relief consisting of an order by a court directing the defendant to perform an act or to refrain from acting in a particular manner.

LIABILITY RULE The distinction between a liability rule and a property rule is that, in the latter, the owner of the property is able to dictate the terms under which development or other activity takes place, whereas, in the former, those carrying out the development or other activity are liable for damages if they do not conform with the wishes of the owner.

MAN-MADE CAPITAL So-called to distinguish it from natural capital.

NATURAL CAPITAL See MAN-MADE CAPITAL.

NORMATIVE ECONOMIC THEORY OF PROPERTY The legal principles which should be adopted in order to secure economically efficient outcomes.

PECUNIARY EXTERNALITY Results from a change in the prices of some inputs or outputs in the economy, for example following a change in demand.

PLANNING GAIN Agreements entered into by local planning authorities and developers for the purpose of permitting the local authority to obtain material benefits or to control aspects of development which, if attempted by attaching conditions to a grant of planning permission, would be *ultra vires*.

POLLUTER PAYS PRINCIPLE States that the cost of measures determined by the public authorities to ensure that the environment is in an acceptable state should be reflected in the price of goods and services which cause pollution in production and/or consumption.

PROPERTY RULE See LIABILITY RULE

PUBLIC GOOD/BAD A pure public good has two salient characteristics: jointness of supply, and the impossibility or inefficiency of excluding others from its consumption, once it has been supplied to some members of the community.

RENT SEEKING The public authorities can help create, increase, or protect a group's monopoly position. In so doing, the monopoly rents of the favoured groups are increased at the expense of the buyers of the group's products or services. The pursuit of these rents by interested parties is known as rent seeking.

STRONG SUSTAINABILITY That form of economic development which leaves all natural capital intact.

SUNK COST A cost which has been incurred and which is irrecoverable.

SUSTAINABLE DEVELOPMENT Development that meets the needs of the present generation without compromising the ability of future generations to meet their own needs.

TECHNOLOGICAL EXTERNALITY An externality which arises from the physical characteristics of the production or consumption process.

TIEBOUT EFFECTS Housing mobility in response to zoning.

TRADABLE DEVELOPMENT RIGHTS Under a system of TDRs, communities manage development by determining areas to be conserved and areas where more concentrated development will be tolerated. TDRs are allocated to landowners whose property lies within designated conservation zones. All future development must be done through the exercise of development rights. Landowners in conservation zones can either exercise rights in development zones or sell their rights to others.

USER COST The benefits forgone by consuming a resource now rather than leaving it for future consumption.

USER PAYS PRINCIPLE The principle that payment for the use of goods and services ought to reflect the full cost of the resources used.

WEAK SUSTAINABILITY Development that leaves the sum total of natural and man-made capital intact.

Commentary

by Malcolm Grant

Introduction

John Corkindale has written a challenging paper. It is a timely contribution to the debate on the future of the planning system that was launched by the Minister's policy statement issued in January this year, *Modernising Planning*.[1] That statement voiced some of the same concerns as he has voiced, and even looked to similar solutions. In particular, it indicated that the Government was willing 'to consider economic instruments and other modern policy tools to help meet the objectives of positive planning' (para. 3), and spoke of the need to make use of instruments such as financial incentives, taxes, subsidies and tradable permits to supplement, rather than replace, the traditional restraint and regulation of town planning (para. 32). In this, it seemed to suggest that economic instruments would be neutral substitutes, as 'modern' tools to be contrasted with the 'old fashioned' tools of command and control.

Corkindale's paper offers a more radical approach: the present system should be scrapped and land development rights should be privatised. I find myself unconvinced both by the diagnosis and the prescription, and unpersuaded by the arguments that lead from one to the other. This is probably unfair: being both a lawyer and an academic imposes on me not one but two levels of cautious scepticism, and a fondness for clear analysis and convincing argumentation. But Corkindale has written more of an 'ideas' paper than a scholarly treatise, and it is not always easy to understand exactly what is being proposed. Although I find its conclusions overstated there are some subordinate arguments which are both interesting and credible, and which deserve further examination.

---

[1] London: Department of the Environment, Transport and the Regions, January 1998.

The Overall Approach

There seem to be three key elements to Corkindale's approach to reform of the British planning system:

(1) the substantive objectives of the planning system;

(2) the process for defining those objectives; and

(3) the tools for achieving those objectives.

It is important to accept that, although related, these are three different issues; and one of the difficulties with the paper is that they tend to become confused. It is one thing to propose new tools to pursue new, more limited, objectives for the planning of land use; it is another thing to understand how existing objectives might be more efficiently pursued through new tools; it is yet another to understand through what political process the objectives are to be redefined and reviewed. It is therefore necessary to separate them for analytical purposes.

The Objectives of the Planning System

It is best to be clear from the beginning that the system of privatising land development rights which the paper proposes is not intended to provide a means of pursuing current planning objectives. It would result in a wholly different planning system with quite different objectives. This is so, notwithstanding the concluding arguments of the paper that, even if the objectives of the current planning system made sense:

> 'there are market-based instruments available which could achieve them more efficiently. After fifty years of the Town and Country Planning Acts, it is now time to privatise land development rights'. (above, p. 57)

But in fact the paper is not at all concerned with pursuing the current objectives, and does not pursue how they could be achieved using market-based instruments. There would, as I understand it (though the distinction is never clearly made), be only two objectives for the new planning system:

(1) the internalisation of technological externalities to the extent required by national legislation; and

(2) the introduction of a charging mechanism to fund the provision of public goods.

These are overlapping but separate objectives. A technological externality resulting from new development may be internalised by requiring the developer to provide some public good, such as the provision of physical infrastructure like roads, drains and sewers; but it may also be internalised by providing non-public goods, such as sound insulation or landscaping or reducing the height of buildings. I have no difficulty in principle with the second objective, though its details are fraught with problems.

The Internalisation of Technological Externalities

Corkindale is clear that 'the land-use planning objectives as currently formulated make little sense', either in form (broad-brush prescriptions lacking performance measures or time-scales) or in substance (for example, the priority that the British planning system has traditionally given to urban containment, without properly evaluating it alongside the higher costs it imposes and the changing functions of cities). He accepts that that there are insuperable practical difficulties in measuring the costs and benefits of the existing arrangements. Nonetheless, he argues, efficiency improvements might be achieved, thereby increasing the net benefits from land use. By the end of the paper, this reappears as a claim that 'nationalised land development rights do not seem to be delivering results in a way which is either cost effective or in line with what people really want', but readers will search in vain for arguments to support this claim. The paper has some discussion of the costs of the system but none of its benefits; and the extent to which the mechanisms of planning law built onto a pluralist democratic system with mediation between national and local objectives already succeed in delivering 'what people really want' is nowhere considered.

There are, of course, many problems with the present process. It is slow and cumbersome and obsessed with detail. Corkindale is right to draw attention to the broad-brush and aspirational character of national policy statements, and the absence from them of any targets or time-scales. But I think he is wrong to ignore almost entirely the policy cascade that seeks to convert those national aspirations into operational local form through regional guidance, strategic plans, area-wide development plans and into development control. Objectives do not exist in a vacuum. They need to be refined into operational form before being pursued, whether through regulatory or market-based instruments.

One of the problems is that the paper fails to spell out clearly how an alternative approach based simply upon the internalisation of technological externalities would operate. Take, for example, the question of the planning implications of the household formation projections. The paper seems to reject the Government's approach, which has been to stimulate debate on the consequences for the future shape, appearance and operations of towns and the countryside of different approaches to accommodating the anticipated growth. Instead, it maintains, a more productive question would have been how the environmental externalities of new housing could be most efficiently internalised. But the paper then avoids addressing that very question, or even attempting to demonstrate how this approach would differ from the Government's own approach. Instead, the argument shifts ground. It moves directly to a discussion of alternative economic mechanisms, and does not return to test their applicability in this policy area.

Yet the assumption is clear: market-based instruments would be more effective in ensuring that technological externalities were internalised at least cost, and the reason this does not occur through the market is the failure of current institutions, particularly private law, to enable private agreements to settle disputes. The paper is also clear that sustainable development requires resort to more efficient mechanisms for achieving environmental goals and ensuring that resources are allocated to the highest-valued use.

But the failure to carry this argument back to the household formation debate is instructive, because the two issues are quite separate: one is about objectives, and the other about instruments. The economic instruments being canvassed are not suited to the Government's broader objectives in addressing the household formation issue. Corkindale concedes that private agreements in the environmental and land-use context are widely held to be impracticable, but maintains that there are nonetheless strong arguments in favour of them. Although he does not spell out what they are, I find myself in agreement with him. There is indeed a good case for improving the mechanisms of private law to enable private agreements to resolve land-use disputes at neighbour nuisance level, and to allow the state to withdraw from its current local land-use mediation rôle and obsession with loft extensions, granny annexes and running businesses from home. As the paper argues, externalities in land-use and development control entail conflicts of interest between the damaged and the damaging parties. When both of those parties are identifiable, and there are no wider interests at stake, a clearer initial allocation of property rights (and not, incidentally, just the presently nationalised development right), coupled to an enhanced negotiating and trading system, could greatly facilitate dispute resolution and economic efficiency.

But these are not, of course, the appropriate instruments for resolving locational issues relating to new growth. Now it may be that Corkindale is right about the economic cost of Britain's containment policy, and that it should now be abandoned in favour of a coalescence of town and country (though it is unfortunate that his discussion of sustainable development does not extend to the sustainability of alternative urban settlement patterns). Nobody should expect that this would be a politically straightforward decision, but were the current objectives of the British planning system simply to be discarded, then the economic instruments he proposes might well suffice – as in the US, where there is no Federal jurisdiction in land use, and even only the most limited State involvement – to meet whatever limited objectives society wished still to pursue. But they are not an alternative means of pursuing current planning objectives.

The Articulation of Objectives

That much at least seems to be accepted in the following passage:

'Of course, the existing planning system would have to be scrapped, but it would be better occupied by a system of TDRs, since such a system would be more likely to accord to the wishes of the local people and would be more responsive to changing economic circumstances.' (above, p. 55)

The proposal is that the internalisation of technological externalities would be better pursued by a system of transferable development rights (TDRs), allowing developers and conservation groups to compete in the market place to acquire additional rights, through which conservation groups could conserve desirable sites. But it seems that TDRs are not to be the sole instrument. Local communities could also vote 'not to have certain types of development on their doorstep at all', and be given more voice to do so by having 'an elected planning committee'.

This is a deeply puzzling proposal. There are, after all, already planning committees in existence within the democratic framework of the local government system. These new committees would apparently be not only outside local government but also outside national policy, which presently is the principal brake on local nimbyism. Their rôle is not explained, but the only likely possibilities seem to be (a) to veto development occurring by using some sort of regulatory control; or (b) to participate, on behalf of those electing them, in the new market for transferable development rights.

If it is to be version (a), the proposal would tend towards even greater cost-free control than the present system, with fewer safeguards against abuse (including corruption). It would also be quite incompatible with the remaining arguments in the paper.

If it is to be version (b), some thought might have been given to how the committees would be resourced, for example, by voluntary contribution (in which case there would be no need for any special machinery, and the choice whether to set up such bodies could be left wholly to local people); or by tax or levy (in which case they become a form of local authority).

Transferable development rights could, of course, operate without any local political structure, entirely as a market-based instrument. Rights would be freely exploited and could be freely traded. But how any of this could be made to 'accord to the wishes of local people' needs to be more clearly spelled out, and this political vacuum in the paper is a major drawback.

The Provision of Public Goods

The second objective, the provision of public goods, would be pursued by a system of development impact fees, along the lines of the Ontario model. There, the paper records, 'developers compensate the Ontario Municipal Board (who are the local planning authority) for the external costs associated with the development'. But this is not strictly the case. The Municipal Board is in fact a quasi-judicial appeals authority, roughly comparable to the Planning Inspectorate. Impact fees are actually levied by local authorities in accordance with provincial legislation, and the developer may challenge the fee in the courts on a question of law, or appeal to the Board on a question of planning.[2] What the paper characterises as 'external costs' in the Ontario context is actually a very narrow concept: it translates roughly into 'public goods'. An impact fee is a proportionate contribution to the off-site capital costs needing to be incurred by public utilities in order to cope with urban growth.

None of this is particularly radical stuff. The model is now applied in several US jurisdictions, and variants have been experimented with in Britain from time to time, making use of the planning obligation powers referred to in the paper.[3] Even the privatised water industry has an impact-fee charging system for infrastructure required in connection with new development,[4] although it is limited by OFWAT to a standard rate in order to avoid cross-subsidisation.

---

[2] See generally D.P. Amborski, 'Impact Fees Canadian Style', in A.C. Nelson (ed.), *Development Impact Fees*, Chicago: Planners Press, 1988, p. 52.

[3] See e.g., *R v Northamptonshire District Council ex p Crest Homes plc* [1994] 3 PLR 47, where the local authority undertook, in consultation with the landowners affected, a calculation of the proportionate contributions to be made by each to physical local infrastructure that would be required in order to accommodate major housing development on their land. However, instead of simply allocating the appropriate proportions of estimated or actual costs, the parties agreed on a formula based upon land value uplift. Despite its resemblance to land value taxation, the Court of Appeal had no hesitation in upholding it.

[4] Water Industry Act 1991, s.146.

Impact fees have considerable potential for introducing some structure, transparency and predictability into planning gain negotiations in this country, but there are several caveats about their use. One is the need to retain a flexibility that reflects changes in economic conditions. This has recently come to a head in Ontario itself, where the Provincial Legislature has enacted a new deregulatory legislative framework[5] which reduces the scope of services eligible for development charges, extends the range of exemptions and adopts new procedures in order to secure greater transparency and openness.[6] Another caveat is that actual incidence is uncertain, and this blurs the extent to which impact fees systems actually do reflect the User Pays Principle; and another is the problem of reconciling a demand-led system of locally-imposed fees with the equalisation principles of British local government finance, in which an increase in locally generated resources may be offset by a reduction in national grant.

Models of Privatisation of Development Rights

It is unfortunate that there is no systematic analysis of the privatisation proposal that lies at the heart of the prescription. There are several possible models, and the paper veers uncertainly between them. The conceptual starting point for each is that, under common law, the ownership of land confers a bundle of different rights, one of which is the right to develop the land provided that it does not adversely affect the property rights of others. It is not an absolute right. It is limited by the law of nuisance, which seeks to provide correlative protection against physical interference with neighbouring land; and it may also be limited by individually negotiated restrictions, such as easements and restrictive covenants, which thereafter run with title to the land.

It was this development right which was effectively nationalised by the Town and Country Planning Act 1947, although the state does not as a result own any physical asset, merely a right of control over private use. This right is

---

[5] Development Charges Act 1997 (Ontario).

[6] Ontario Ministry of Municipal Affairs and Housing News Release, 2 March 1998.

'privatised' on a case-by-case basis by the grant of planning permission, but this is a limited divesting: it relates only to a specific development proposal, and local planning authorities tend to maintain tight controls over its execution and subsequent use. It is also 'privatised', though to a limited extent, by general instruments of national effect such as the General Permitted Development Order[7] and the Use Classes Order.[8]

It is important to appreciate that these arrangements are quite different from those in almost every other country in the world, and particularly the USA where much of the experimentation with TDRs has taken place. In the US, the right to develop is protected, as a property right, by the Fifth Amendment to the US Constitution, and the US Supreme Court has been taking an increasingly strong line against regulatory interference with it.[9] Against a background that is hostile to interference with vested property rights, TDRs provide a convenient means of compensating landowners for forgoing their development rights. Landowners may have acquired their land in expectation of being entitled to develop it, and it is appropriate that they should be compensated for the removal of that expectation. But the design of TDRs is not straightforward. If trading is to be promoted, there needs to be an initial restriction of the extent of the rights, and a use restriction on their exploitation. If every landowner has an unlimited right to develop, there is no incentive for other

---

[7] Town and Country Planning (General Permitted Development) Order 1995 (SI 1995 No. 418).

[8] Town and Country Planning (Use Classes) Order 1987 (SI 1987 No. 764).

[9] See e.g., *Nollan v California Coastal Commission* (1987) 483 US 825; *First English Evangelical Lutheran Church v County of Los Angeles* (1987) 482 US 304, both discussed in D. Callies and M. Grant, 'Paying for growth and planning gain: an Anglo-American Comparison of Development Conditions, Impact Fees and Development Agreements', 23 Urb Law 221 (1991) and reproduced in Robert H. Freilich and David W. Bushek (eds.), *Exactions, Impact Fees and Dedications*, American Bar Association (1995); and *Lucas v South Carolina Coastal Council* (1992) 112 SCt 2886; *Dolan v City of Tigard* (1995), both discussed in M. Grant, 'If Tigard were an English City', in D. Callies (ed.), *Takings: Land Development Conditions and Regulatory Takings after Dolan and Lucas* (American Bar Association, 1996). The latest foray looks likely to come with *Del Monte Dunes at Monterey, Ltd. v. City Of Monterey*, 95 F.3d 1422 (9th Cir. 1996), which the Supreme Court has now accepted for review in the current session of the Court.

landowners to acquire rights from those whose land is to be protected from development. And if there is no limit on the rights that an owner can acquire and exploit on his land, then there will be negative externalities for his neighbours. So the initial allocation of rights must necessarily be restricted by a floor and a ceiling.

I take 'privatisation' in Corkindale's paper to mean the process by which the state might divest itself of its right to control private land development. There are at least four models:

(1) *Deregulation*: under this model, controls are simply lifted, with the effect that the rights that previously were restricted simply 'vest' in the landowner for the time being. Examples include the creation of Class B1 under the Use Classes Order in 1987, which brought together light industrial, office and research and development uses. The objective of such deregulation is to secure greater liberalisation of the market. No price is charged by the state, and it is difficult to see how it could be when landowners do not presently pay a price for the grant of planning permission on an application. Yet, once development rights are surrendered in this way, they become part of the landowner's bundle of property rights, and, upon the coming into force of the Human Rights Bill, they may well be protected as such from uncompensated expropriation.[10] Hence the state, having surrendered its controls, might be forced to buy them back as transferable development rights in order to secure its international obligations in relation, for example, to wetlands and habitat protection.[11] Deregulation may be an entirely appropriate way for the state to privatise land development rights at the margin, but it needs to be stressed that a simple lifting of

---

[10] By virtue of Article 1 of the First Protocol. It was accepted last year by the High Court in *R v North Lincolnshire Council, ex parte Horticultural and Garden Products Sales (Humberside) Ltd* (Lightman J; 31 July, 1997) that a planning permission constituted a property right *prima facie* protected by the European Convention (which the Human Rights Bill will translate into national law), though on the facts its uncompensated revocation was within the state's margin of appreciation under the Convention.

[11] Notably under Council Directive 92/43/EEC on the conservation of natural habitats and of wild fauna and flora.

planning controls would have a dramatic impact on the market. Land suitable for development has a value which reflects that fact, whether or not it yet has planning permission. For the past 50 years, transactions in development land in Britain have taken place on the assumption that development rights did not transfer with the land unless, until, and to the extent that, planning permission was granted for development. Where permission has not been granted, but the land may be suitable for development in the future, appropriate discounting is applied. Hence the wholesale surrender by the state of development rights would result in a levelling out in price between land allocated for development (including that already developed) and land not allocated. The impact would be felt both as an uplift in demand for sites presently protected, such as land within a green belt; and as a downturn in value for sites presently allocated for development. A more modest approach to privatisation would have a more modest economic effect. It might, for example, substitute new obligations (see further below). Or it might apply only to certain types of land (or, equally, not apply at all to certain types of land, such as protected habitats). But such an approach begs the question of how and by whom the limits are to be set (for example, through zoning or TDRs); whether they are to be permanent or reviewable (and if so, by whom: the political dimension again); and the unfairness as between landowners which would be the consequence of such discriminatory deregulation.

(2) *Sell-off*: under the 'conventional' privatisation model of the past 18 years, a state-owned asset such as a public utility is transferred first to a company whose share capital is then floated on the stock exchange, without restrictions on purchase or subsequent sale of shares, and the Government gets the best price available under the flotation arrangements. It is clear that this is not an appropriate model for the privatisation of development rights because they are always site-specific, even if, as Corkindale proposes, they are

subsequently to become tradable. Only then do they become commodities for which there may be a general market.

(3) *Auction:* a similar problem arises with this approach, which was mooted several years ago by Peter Hall, but essentially involves requiring developers to obtain both a planning permission and the necessary development rights, perhaps by Treasury allocation.

(4) *Substitution*: under this model, there is a resettlement of rights. This seems to be closest to what Corkindale is proposing. The existing system would not be replaced by a vacuum, but the space would instead be better occupied by a system of TDRs 'since such a system would be more likely to accord to the wishes of local people and would be more responsive to changing economic circumstances', and 'break down the divisive and unhelpful perception . . . that a rigid distinction between the urban and the rural should be maintained'. In place of the present discretionary system of development control, there might be substituted a system of zoning upon which transferable development rights could be founded. Proponents of zoning point to the certainty that it affords. Development rights are defined for each zone, and this helps to provide a foundation for trading. The New York model is often cited, with its limited system of transferable development rights which permits the transfer of density allowances between sites,[12] and there are other examples cited in the paper. But in truth there are almost as many models of zoning as there are local jurisdictions in North America, and a great range of experience. In some – Hawaii, for example – 'as of right' development has almost entirely disappeared in favour of discretionary control; and Florida even has a General Development Order. But zoning has its disadvantages. As Cullingworth observes:

'It is important to stress that zoning is an inherently rigid instrument. This remains so in spite of the extraordinary ingenuity which has been displayed in adapting it to the real moving world;

---

[12] See for example *Penn Central Transportation v City of New York* (1978) 438 US 104.

and in this rigidity lies its enormous popular appeal. The planning ideal of flexibility is anathema to protectionist home owners. Rigidity provides a degree of certainty and security. But zoning is not planning: it is a restricted instrument for districting.'[13]

Corkindale implicitly accepts these criticisms, and suggests a reorientation of focus of zoning, onto the actual externalities generated by a particular land use, rather than the use itself. If zoning were to be the ideal model, then this would be a sensible modification of it, though it undermines the capacity of the zoning model for providing a sharper definition of property rights. Environmental externalities from modern industrial uses are far more limited than those for which zoning – based on the separation of incompatible land uses – was originally designed. But zoning still provides a means of reducing other externalities, such as heavy traffic, by excluding even benign non-residential land uses from residential areas. In fact, one of the best examples of the 'effects-based' approach to zoning that the paper espouses exists already in this country with Class B1 of the Use Classes Order, which allows unrestricted changes of use between light industrial, office and R&D uses, provided they are compatible with the amenities of a residential area.

TDRs are an attempt to overcome some of the rigidity that flows from a general system of vested rights.[14] Moreover, actual experience with TDRs is very limited because of their potentially dramatic physical redistributive effect.[15] They tend to be

---

[13] Barry Cullingworth, *Planning in the USA: Policies, issues and processes*, London and New York: Routledge, 1997, p. 63.

[14] As opposed to the limited system of vested rights under British planning law: expectations based on the development plans or other material considerations only crystallise into legal rights in this country upon the grant of planning permission, and there is generally a five-year period for their implementation, otherwise they lapse. During that period, and following implementation, the rights are removable only in accordance with a specified procedure and with compensation for all losses. In a typical US zoning system, the rights are defined by the zoning ordinance, but they may be varied, and some states have a 'late vesting' rule which allows zoning to be changed right up to the time that construction work commences.

[15] There are few active TDR programmes in operation in the US, though many jurisdictions have them in their legislation. The best known, in addition to the Pinelands Reserve example cited by Corkindale, is a programme in Montgomery

supported by the neighbours of a 'sending area' and resisted by neighbours of a 'receiving area'. In fact, the more successful model in the US has that of purchase of development rights (PDR) where development rights are acquired by local or state governments, and the landowner signs a conservation easement that runs with the land; but instead of being used elsewhere, the rights are simply retired. Hence the state acquires development rights, not by nationalisation but by negotiation. To propose such a scheme here would ironically involve the state either ceding the development rights which it presently controls and then buying them back, or adopting a discriminatory and unequal approach to privatisation in the first place.

Conclusions

It follows that I remain unconvinced of the central thesis of Corkindale's paper. I do not believe that the arguments are sufficiently robust to support the bold claims that are made for the privatisation of land development rights, on whatever of the models I have analysed above.

But that is not to say that there is no rôle for market-based instruments in pursuing various objectives of the British planning system, nor even that those objectives do not themselves require further review. There are two areas in particular where such an approach should be welcomed.

The first is in relation to local neighbourhood land-use conflicts, where the planning system is often used as an exceptionally heavy instrument to resolve disputes that could be more effectively dealt with through a private property system. Instead of considering whether to extend planning control to the planting of *leylandii*, for example, there should be a sharper articulation of inter-neighbour property rights along Coasian lines, and appropriate legal institutions for resolving disputes.

The second area is in relation to the private funding of public goods in connection with new development. This is a wide issue, which ranges from one extreme to the taxation of betterment, and at the other to user charges. Because of the accusations of impropriety that have sometimes been levelled against our

---

County, Maryland, which has secured over 43,000 acres of farmland from development.

present system of planning gain, most recently by the Nolan Committee,[16] successive governments have preferred to try to limit the practice by exhortative advice, and have abdicated responsibility for evaluating how best to charge back to developers/landowners the external costs generated by their development, in a way which is fair, transparent and predictable. This remains a troubling instance of institutional failure in the British planning system.

---

[16] *Standards of Conduct in Local Government in England*, Cm. 3702, 1997.

Commentary

by Mark Pennington

In a recent article for *The Times* newspaper,[1] the Secretary of State for the Environment, Transport and the Regions, John Prescott, MP, spoke of the successes of the British Town and Country Planning system, which through the introduction of Green Belts and National Parks, he claimed, 'has done so much to protect the countryside – one of our great national assets'. In the same article, however, Mr Prescott spoke also of the pressing need to modernise the planning system, creating a régime which is 'less rigid, more democratic and more sustainable'. Unfortunately, it is this latter statement which exposes the underlying reality of planning in Britain today.

As an ageing relic of Attlee's post-war nationalisation programme, the British land-use planning system typifies the hallmark failures of similar socialist-inspired schemes. Numerous studies have documented institutional inertia in the system, its unresponsiveness to changing lifestyle patterns and consumer demands and the stifling effects of bureaucratic red tape on economic growth.[2] Additional studies have highlighted the capture of the regulatory régime by interested parties. In the recent furore over the future of Green Belts, for example, The Council for the Protection of Rural England may have claimed that it is the guardian of the national environmental heritage, but that its members' property values have been enhanced by Green Belts has led many to question the extent of this apparent altruism.[3] Finally, there is the mounting burden to the taxpayer of continuing to operate the administrative bureaucracy.

---

[1] *The Times*, 26 January, 1998.

[2] See for example J. Simmie, (1993) *Planning at the Crossroads*, London: UCL Press, 1993, and G. Cherry, *Town Planning in Britain Since 1900*, Oxford: Basil Blackwell, 1996.

[3] See, for example, A. Evans, 'Rabbit Hutches on Postage Stamps: Planning Development & Political Economy', *Urban Studies*, Vol.28, No.6, 1991, pp. 853-70.

In the last 20 years real expenditure has increased three fold (£1.5 billion), but the number of development applications processed by planners has barely increased at all, suggesting that town and country planning is not the most productive of government activities.[4]

In spite of these manifest failings, there is little evidence to suggest that meaningful reform is on the horizon. Politicians of all parties are fond of criticising the planning system but their proposals amount to little more than institutional tinkering. If, by implication of Mr Prescott's remarks, land-use planning has for half a century been rigid, undemocratic and unsustainable – why should it be capable of a dramatic transformation now? In short, the inefficiencies of the British planning system stem from fundamental institutional defects which are central to its very nature. First and foremost amongst these is the nationalisation of development rights, a socialist arrangement which is surely ripe for abolition.

It is this central question of how to move away from a nationalised planning system and to develop an alternative, more efficient approach to the management of land-use change which John Corkindale examines in this stimulating paper. For too long apologists for the *status quo* have defended inefficient planning practices on the feeble grounds that they are an indispensable component of environmental protection in a modern industrial society. As John Corkindale argues, however, 'Public land-use planning is not the only mechanism available for internalising externalities and providing public goods' (p. 32). Property rights solutions, in particular, can provide a cheaper, more efficient and more responsive alternative for local communities.

The favoured option advanced in this paper is a system of tradable development rights. Just as tradable permits in the field of air pollution control have proved a more flexible and efficient method of coping with externalities than traditional command and control approaches, so, according to John Corkindale, a system of tradable land development rights could bring about similar efficiency gains. The principal advantage of such a

---

[4] See M. Pennington, 'Budgets, Bureaucrats and the Containment of Urban England', *Environmental Politics*, Vol.6, No.4, 1997, pp.76-107.

scheme would result from a reduction in the cumbersome administrative bureaucracy which currently regulates the development of land. By providing development credits for landowners who simultaneously engage in environmental protection, incentives would be more closely geared towards the goals of both development and conservation.

John Corkindale's proposal would mark a radical innovation in the way land-use change is managed in Britain and may indeed represent an improvement on the existing bureaucratic régime. It is not clear, however, that the proposals advanced in this paper should actually be described as an example of privatisation, much less a 'free market' approach to land-use control. Tradable permit schemes may well be considerably better than more typical command and control methods of environmental protection, but they are only a *market-like* alternative. As Anderson and Leal have pointed out, such schemes still require a political determination of the level of environmental protection desired and as such are open to two important critiques which lie at the heart of the case for a still more radical 'free market environmentalism'.[5]

The first of these critiques refers to the calculational difficulties and 'knowledge problems' associated with central planning. As Hayek and the Austrian school have argued, the preferences of individual consumers are subjective and are incapable of being measured by an outside observer.[6] It is only in situations of actual choice that preferences are revealed and only when people decide to exchange one thing for another (an amount of money for a scenic view, for example) that relative weights can be assigned to these preferences. Thus, in the absence of a genuine market where property rights are assigned, there is no way for government planners to know how much evironmental protection is actually desired. It is disappointing, therefore, that John Corkindale advocates the adoption of 'environmental evaluation techniques' as an aid to planning

---

[5] T. Anderson, and D. Leal , *Free Market Environmentalism*, San Francisco: Pacific Research Institute for Public Policy, 1991.

[6] F. A. Hayek, 'The Use of Knowledge in Society', *American Economic Review*, Vol. 35, No.4, 1948, pp. 519-30.

decisions. Such guesswork is an inherently subjective process and it is precisely for this reason that the results of cost/benefit analyses and environmental impact assessments are never taken seriously by planners themselves. This same arbitrariness would apply when planners decide on the environmental objectives of the system proposed by John Corkindale and engage in the allocation of land development permits.

The second critique derived from public choice theory points to the inherent tendency towards 'government failure' if the allocation of property rights is left to politicians and bureaucrats.[7] When interest groups and bureaucrats capture the political process, voters have insufficient incentives to discipline mismanagement because the costs are so widely spread among taxpayers, none of whom can have a decisive influence on the result of an election. These are the very processes which have led to many of the problems witnessed in today's planning system and, it can be argued, might have undue influence on a system of tradable permits. Thus, it is far from obvious that the proposals advanced here would remove the problem of interest group 'capture' and would not require an enormous administrative bureaucracy to supervise the allocation of the permits.

The ultimate solution to these problems is to have the *allocation of property rights and hence the level of environmental protection itself determined in the market* and thus to confine the rôle of the state to the enforcement of contractual agreements made between private parties. The best example of such property rights entrepreneurship in a land-use context is the use of restrictive covenants enforced under the common law. In these circumstances, developers specify in contracts the particular activities which are to be permitted with respect to a particular set of properties for sale, in order to internalise externalities and capture the rents through higher asset prices. At Big Sky Valley in Montana, for example, developers bought up an entire mountain valley, which they then subdivided, selling tracts with restrictive covenants allowing only aesthetically acceptable

---

[7] See for example, James Buchanan et al., *The Economics of Politics*, IEA Readings 18, IEA, London, 1978.

development.[8] Through a variety of similar private solutions (with some areas having strict contractual requirements and others operating free of controls), it is possible for consumers to reveal their demands for environmental protection and for entrepreneurs to be sensitive to different individual preferences in a competitive market context.[9] In so doing, the calculational difficulties afflicting central planning and the public choice problems associated with political management are effectively removed. Whilst there are limits to such approaches where transactions costs are insurmountable, as in the case of atmospheric pollution control, such problems are less significant for stationary resources such as land and are relatively minor when compared to the transactions costs experienced in the administration of land-use planning.

The above remarks should not be seen to detract from John Corkindale's paper. On the contrary, the proposals made are a radical and innovative contribution to the debate on the future of land management in Britain and should be welcomed on these grounds alone. Moreover, in putting a persuasive case for a market-like system of tradable development rights and placing private property rights solutions firmly on the policy agenda, this analysis may hasten the arrival of a genuinely free market system. In so far as John Corkindale's paper pushes us towards this goal, it is to be heartily recommended.

---

[8] R. Stroup, 'Rescuing Yellowstone From Politics: Expanding Parks While Reducing Conflicts', in J. Baden and D. Leal, *The Yellowstone Primer*, San Francisco: Pacific Research Institute for Public Policy, 1990.

[9] See M. Pennington, *Conservation and the Countryside: By Quango or Market?*, IEA Studies on the Environment, No. 6, London: Institute of Economic Affairs, 1996, for a more detailed exposition.